Dedicated

To my wife Eileen
without whom I couldn't exist
and to the memory of my donor
without whom I wouldn't exist

Memoirs Of An Irish Journalist

IT'S ALL NEWS TO ME

BY KEVIN FARRELL

Paperweight

First published in 2011 by Paperweight Publications, Level 4, Building 5, Dundrum Townhouse Centre, Dublin 16, Ireland.

The right of Kevin Farrell to be identified as the author of this work has been asserted in accordance with the Copyright, Designs and Patents Act 1988.

ISBN 9780956913494

Printed and bound by CPI Group
(UK) Ltd, Croydon, CR0 4YY

Paperweight Publishing Group, Level 4, Building 5,
Dundrum Townhouse Centre, Dublin 16, Ireland.

HYPERLINK "http://www.paperweightpublications.ie" www.paperweight-publications.ie

Kevin Farrell is a senior journalist with The Irish Daily Star. He is married to Eileen and they live in Edenderry. They have two sons, a daughter and four grandchildren.

Edited by Des Gibson
Designed by Ciaran Farren
For Paperweight Publications

Acknowledgements

THERE are so many people to thank in connection with this publication that it would be impossible to mention them all.

However, I must thank *Irish Daily Star* Editor Gerard Colleran for his encouragement from the moment I told him about my desire to pen this book. As a reporter with the *Irish Daily Star* I have enjoyed working under him during a period in which he brought the paper to new heights by making it Ireland's top selling daily tabloid.

The first few drafts of this publication reflected the real me in that they were all over the place. That was when I called in my old friend of more than 25 years, former *Sunday World* news editor Sean Boyne. With numerous books to his credit, Sean's experience soon whipped my efforts into shape. He worked tirelessly to get everything ready for the publishers and without him I doubt if I would have ever completed the task. To an old and loyal friend, *"Thank you Sean."*

Sincere thanks to another good friend of many years, Eddie Rowley, who wrote the Foreword. Thanks, also, to Des Gibson of Paperweight Publications, who brought it all to finality. Finally, to anyone who helped me in any way during my work on the book, a big thank you.

Foreword

AS a senior reporter with *The Star* newspaper, Kevin Farrell has covered some of the country's biggest stories and interviewed a multitude of larger-than-life characters.

But Kevin is a colourful and interesting personality in his own right, and here he has a fascinating life story to tell.

Not least is his gripping account of the fearful months spent on the invisible death row, as he waited on the call to have a life-saving liver transplant while at the same time undergoing tre atment for a cancerous tumour. The call would eventually come, and Kevin has survived to tell his inspiring tale.

That personal battle alone could provide a roller coaster drama for an entire book, but this is Kevin Farrell, a man who has packed so many more experiences into his life.

There was the time, for instance, when *The Star* newspaper despatched him to the Midlands to report on the story of a missing child — only for Kevin to become the hero of the moment when he found the bewildered little girl himself on a lonely country road while investigating the story. A man was later apprehended and convicted of the abduction of the child.

As a newspaperman, Kevin is the quintessential, old-school journalist with a contact in every city, town, parish and backwater of Ireland. When a story broke, Kevin got to the heart of it in an instant with a quick phone call. I've heard young reporters on the paper describe him as *"a legend"*.

I've personally known Kevin since I was a teenager writing local notes for the Mullingar-based *Topic* newspaper. Kevin was their reporter in Offaly, and was then famous for penning a satirical, gossipy column, *Backstage*, using the pseudonym *'Nivek'*.

I started doing a version of it in the *'Kinnegad Notes'* and Kevin looked me up to check me out. That was back in the 1970s and we've been friends ever since. Kevin encouraged and inspired me when I went into journalism and down the road we would both end up in Dublin on national papers — he with *The Star*, and I with the *Sunday World*, where he had also been a journalist for many years, working under our then news editor Sean Boyne.

Apart from our love of newspapers, we also share a passion for the world of entertainment. Before his journalistic career, Kevin managed a kid called Michael Landers. Known as *'The Boy Wonder,'* he was a sensation on the showband scene until the law intervened. I'll let Kevin tell the rest of that story.

As the entertainment manager of The Copper Beech in Edenderry, Kevin worked with some of the biggest names in the business, from Joe Dolan to Brendan Grace to a young Johnny Logan and an even younger Barry McGuigan.

He even penned and recorded his own record, *A Tribute To Michael O'Hehir*! It was later recorded by Jack Allen, a brother of Tony Allen of Foster & Allen and also Tom Allen, AKA T.R. Dallas.

By the end of the book, you'd have to say Kevin Farrell's

life is stranger than that of any fictional character. And a hell of a lot more interesting. And that's before he goes reelin' in the years by dipping into some of the interesting news events he's covered through the decades.

Kevin, of course, hasn't forgotten where he came from and his memories and anecdotes from humble beginnings in the Midlands paint a vivid, colourful, rich picture of times past in Ireland.

This book is a gem that will be thoroughly enjoyed by readers at home, as well as Irish people scattered around the globe.

- Eddie Rowley, Showbiz Editor in the Sunday World

Introduction

I BEGAN my working life serving in a hardware shop in my native Edenderry, County Offaly. I was not suited to the work and I did not enjoy it. While still a teenager I began promoting dances as a sideline and enjoyed some success. Finally, in October 1967, I bade farewell to the hardware trade and hung up my brown shop coat. I decided to devote myself to the more glamorous world of show business and went on to encounter an array of marvellous characters from the Irish showband world, and the odd chancer as well.

After a few years I made the transition into what some regard as a branch of show business, journalism, and greatly enjoyed working on news stories at home and abroad. My vacancy in the hardware shop was filled by a young lad from nearby Rhode called Seamus Darby. He even took my shop coat, and was welcome to it. Seamus was destined to go down in Irish sporting history for scoring the goal that won Offaly an All-Ireland and deprived Kerry of a Five-in-a-Row victory. Seamus is among the characters who figure significantly in this memoir that you are about to read.

Show business and journalism pose their own challenges

for those involved in these occupations, but they were nothing in comparison to the health challenge I faced in recent years while working for the *Irish Daily Star* newspaper in Dublin. Struck down with a cancerous tumour on my liver, I was told I needed a liver transplant. Thankfully, the operation was a success and I was given a new lease of life. I hope my story will help boost the morale of others who are also facing into a transplant operation.

I have had a varied career, have lived an eventful life and, in terms of health, came close to the edge, but survived. Every day has been a different journey, a new challenge. I guess you could say that it's all been news to me...

CHAPTER 1

A New Lease Of Life

BEFORE going to work at the *Irish Daily Star* newspaper on the morning of December 27, 2004, I had to visit my younger brother Seamus at St Vincent's Hospital in Dublin. He had undergone a liver transplant operation and I must admit I wasn't exactly looking forward to seeing him so soon after surgery, although we had been told that the transplant had gone well.

When his wife Mary walked me to his bedside I got the shock of my life. Had I been alone I would have passed by him ten times without recognising him. All those tubes and wires! My God, this wasn't natural. In truth, I was thrilled that the visit had to be for a minute or two. It was long enough for me. I was so traumatised that I lost my way on that short journey between the hospital at Elm Park and our office in Terenure, on the south side of Dublin. I remember saying to myself that if I had to face the same situation I would prefer to die than undergo such surgery. When I entered the newsroom later that morning my colleague Catherine Halloran on the newsdesk asked me if I'd seen a ghost or if it was just a bad hangover.

I did damn-all work that day. I just couldn't concentrate on anything. I was very conscious of the fact that I was also attending a consultant for a liver ailment. The consultant had told me that my liver was functioning well. Indeed, he said it was working better than it should be, and I was thrilled.

But I was thinking, *'what if it deteriorates?'* It didn't bear thinking about. My brother Seamus made a fantastic recovery, but the word *"transplant"* still put a shiver up my spine. No way would I entertain one. No way! I'll opt to meet my Maker, I thought. I was also conscious that my older brother Liam had passed away with a similar illness at the old Adelaide Hospital in Dublin back in 1988.

****

It was pouring rain when I came out of the church in Ballinamore, County Leitrim on a cold wet Friday in December 2008. I had just attended the funeral Mass for Mrs Patricia Williams, mother of Paul Williams, the noted crime correspondent and author. I had decided to leave town immediately before any invitations to booze might be on offer. As I made the long journey towards home I stopped-off in Mohill and went into a pub there to grab a bowl of soup and a sandwich. Suddenly I discovered I wasn't that hungry. But the grub had been ordered so I waited. I took three or four spoonfuls of soup and ate half a sandwich before deciding to continue my journey home.

But when I went out of the pub I couldn't remember where I had parked my car. It upset me because I was aware that memory loss was part of liver psoriasis, and I had remembered my brother Seamus had suffered a bout or two of memory loss prior to his transplant. It also struck me that approximately two months previously on my way home from the office in

Terenure I had driven around the Spawell roundabout three times before I finally got onto the M50 motorway. I sat on a window sill in Mohill as the rain bucketed down and eventually I remembered the direction from which I had walked after parking. I eventually found my car and drove home.

Later that night I enjoyed a fabulous roast chicken dinner with roast potatoes, but within an hour I felt sick. I seldom suffer from an upset tummy and the only time I can ever remember actually vomiting would be from beer, and that was way back when I was only serving my time to our national pastime. I had been in my early 20s before I actually broke my Pioneer total abstinence pledge. That night after the funeral I went to bed some time after midnight but I was only minutes in bed when I had to run to the bathroom. I got sick and alarm bells started to ring when I noticed that I was throwing up blood. Not a lot, but enough to frighten the shit out of me. I had an idea of what was happening. I had been warned that varices (veins) in my oesophagus could burst and I had been prescribed medication to prevent such a happening only weeks earlier.

The following morning I attended my GP, Dr Philip Brady. He has been my saviour and rock now for many years and I'm so lucky to have him. I knew by him that morning that he was very concerned and he warned me that if things didn't improve during the day I should present myself at the Accident and Emergency department of the Midlands Regional Hospital at Tullamore. Things didn't improve and I found myself arriving at Tullamore Hospital at 7.20pm on Saturday, December 20, and being finally admitted some time after five o'clock the following morning. I was left sitting shivering and feeling absolutely terrible for 10 hours. It was anything but a busy Saturday night at the A&E department, so what delayed my admission is something I will never know, and the HSE don't answer such queries. As Eamon Dunphy once said of the HSE: *"They defend themselves with a viciousness."*

On Sunday morning, December 21, I was introduced to Geraldine McCormack, a consultant who specialises in liver problems. I had been told on more than one occasion during the previous 12 months to go and see her. I was delighted that she was on duty and she had treated my brother Seamus, so she had an idea of what she was dealing with. I was taken to theatre where I had that ugly procedure of an endoscopy followed by what they term *"banding of the varices"*. It is exactly what is says on the tin. It is a procedure where they tie up the burst varices with elastic or rubber bands. I felt very, very sick for the remainder of that day and for a further two or three days I wasn't feeling great. I can recall having just jelly and ice cream on Christmas Day. Matters improved, but on New Year's Eve I was transferred to St Vincent's Hospital. At Vincent's they examined the banding of the varices that had been carried out at Tullamore and did some other tests as well. I will always remember being transferred to St Vincent's that day. I could picture all the people who were planning to ring in the New Year and here was I in the back of an ambulance with its siren blaring as we sped up the N4 and on to the M50.

That terrifying word *"transplant"* had again entered my mind and I thought all I could do now was pray. I was so relieved a few days later at Vincent's when a young doctor arrived in. I can still see him leaning against the wall and flicking his pen between his fingers as he gazed at my chart and tests results. *"You know your liver is not that bad at all,"* he said.

"Does that mean no transplant?" I asked.

"Well, certainly not at the moment anyway," he replied.

Jaysus, I could have kissed him I was that thrilled. Finally I could relax.

After five days in St Vincent's I was allowed home and I had visions of returning to work after a couple of weeks. But within a day of coming home from St Vincent's I suffered memory loss once more. I was turning day into night and vice versa. My wife Eileen found me frying rashers at 4am (and the thing is, we always grill) while on another morning at 3.30am I was re-arranging dishes in the dishwasher. Dr Brady was phoned and after talking to me for a few minutes an ambulance was summoned to take me back to Tullamore Hospital. I spent another four or five days there.

In March 2009, Dr Geraldine McCormack ordered an MRI scan and I was apprehensive when I got word a week later that she wanted to see me. I went over to see her alone. It was the first time that Eileen or another family member did not accompany me. Eileen was babysitting and was upset that she couldn't be with me. Dr McCormack looked across the desk at me and I knew something was wrong when she said, "*Oh, is your wife not here? That's a pity.*" Rustling some papers on her desk she looked straight at me said, "*Kevin, I'm really sorry but I have detected a tumour on your liver. I cannot say for certain how serious it is, but I'm referring you to Professor McCormack in St Vincent's. I'm really, really sorry.*"

It was tough news to get but, in fairness to the doctor, she handled it as best as she could in the circumstances. I left the building and walked down the town of Tullamore. On the way I stopped on the Kilbeggan Bridge and stared into the stagnant waters of the Grand Canal. I was gutted. Having kicked the habit of 70 cigarettes a day on September 21, 1989, I had often said to myself how ironic it would be if I died from cancer after all I had suffered giving them up. I decided to phone Eileen and there was only one thing to do. Tell the truth, the complete truth. Eileen was so upset that she insisted on coming over to Tullamore and meeting Dr McCormack herself. We had another brief meeting with her in the afternoon during which she disclosed the same information that she had given me earlier. At least now Eileen was getting it from the horse's mouth, and this was so important for her.

I went to St Vincent's Private Hospital for a more specific scan and about three weeks later I found myself sitting in front of Professor Aidan McCormack at the Liver Clinic in St Vincent's. He was armed with the scan results. He looked across his desk and said, *"I'm afraid the scan showed up a tumour. It is 2.9cm and hopefully it won't get any bigger."* Professor McCormack said that if it increased to 5cm it was all over for me.

He went on to say that it was not possible to remove it. If they did, I would probably suffer liver failure. He explained that the only hope was a liver transplant. The day that I dreaded, and prayed would never come, had now arrived. I did my best to stay calm. Professor McCormack explained that if I agreed to a transplant I would have to be assessed for such a procedure. When I asked him when that assessment would be likely to take place he replied, *"In about ten minutes."*

As we left Professor McCormack's room there was little conversation between Eileen and myself. I had often wondered how one would react if told they had cancer. Realistically, it didn't bear thinking about so I used to always dismiss it as fast as I'd think of it. Not now though. It's here. *'You have cancer, Kevin. Face it man!'* We just looked at each other. No words spoken. The assessment took about three visits to St Vincent's Hospital and I was eventually deemed fit for surgery and placed on the official liver transplant list on June 2, 2009.

I reflected on how my memory had been affected by my illness. I didn't know at the time why I had suffered a memory loss when I came out of that pub in Mohill on December 18, 2008, nor did I know why I had suffered an even worse bout of it when I came home from my first stay in St Vincent's in January 2009. After I was re-admitted to Tullamore Hospital in January 2009 suffering from loss of memory the doctor quizzed me about different things in an attempt to establish how far gone I was. We differed over what day of the week it was and I got annoyed with him when he told me it was Saturday, with me insisting it was Tuesday.

"Who is the Taoiseach?" asked the doctor.

"Brian Cowen... for now," I replied. The doctor grinned.

Later in the year when St Vincent's presented me with a booklet on patients undergoing liver transplant assessment, I was to learn fully what was going on. I also learned about sleep reversal. This was something I had been suffering from for quite a long time and I was blaming it on everything except a liver ailment. I usually went to bed around 11pm. I slept for the first hour then lay awake until around 5am. When the alarm went off at 7.30am I had to drag myself out the bed and make the journey to work in Terenure. By 4pm each I day I was totally drained.

Under the heading *'Confusion'* in this little booklet I learned that this memory lapse and Sleep Reversal is caused by a build-up of toxins in the blood that the liver is unable to break down. It occurs mainly as a result of constipation, infection or bleeding anywhere in the gut. There are four varying grades of confusion. It can present as a general slowing of mental thoughts or minor memory lapses, which only family or medical staff may notice, all the way to the development of a coma. Confusion is resolved by treatment of the underlying problem. It is only now I realise that some of my editors must have noticed some deterioration in my work. Looking back now I can remember stupid mistakes and bouts of forgetfulness, the latter being something I never suffered from until recent years. I used put it down to age, and maybe too many pints of beer along the way.

On June 2, 2009, the Hospital Coordinator at St Vincent's summoned the entire family to a meeting after it had been decided that I was a fit candidate for a liver transplant. We were taken to a room just across the road from the main hospital and I can remember it was a blistering hot day. So hot, in fact, that both my sons broke into sweats with the youngest leaving before the gory details of what was going to happen to me were delivered by that efficient Coordinator. My daughter Sinead listened attentively as did my wife Eileen but they told me afterwards that I just stared up to the ceiling.

I cannot remember everything of what the Coordinator told us except that she concluded her talk with the words, *"As and from now you are officially on the list."* That hit home.

We heard what would happen immediately after I arrived in the operating theatre. They would transfer me from the bed to the operating table. As it happened I made the journey to the theatre in a wheelchair. We were told how a heart monitor would be attached and a blood pressure cuff would be placed on my arm and a probe placed on my finger. They put a drip called a cannula in a vein in the back of your hand and a sharp dose of drugs to make you sleep. Once they get you asleep, a tube is placed into your lungs attached to a ventilator and it takes over the work of your lungs. Two tubes are shoved up your nose to ensure that your stomach does not become full of air during the surgery and to provide nutrition in the initial days after surgery. Several drips are placed in your neck, generally on the right-hand side. Drips are also placed on both wrists to provide a more accurate measurement of your blood pressure and to allow blood samples to be taken throughout your surgery. A tube is placed in your bladder to drain away urine and to allow the team to monitor your kidney functions. Your legs and arms are wrapped in cotton wool to keep you warm during surgery. I just wished I had of asked one of the team to take a picture of me at this stage!

The medical people refer to the above procedures as the

"anaesthetic phase" and now that they have you hooked to more wires than the ESB power plant in Moneypoint, they are ready to gut you. This is where it gets a bit technical and I wasn't too interested in hearing or reading about it, but they are anxious that you should know everything that is going to happen. After all it is YOUR life that is in their hands.

An incision is made either in the shape of the Mercedes-Benz symbol (a sort of 'Y' upside down) or an 'L' shape, only try and imagine an 'L' backwards. That is the one I had and I still cannot bring myself to look at it.

To remove your diseased liver the surgeons must identify the blood vessels bringing blood to and from the liver and the bile duct which takes bile from the liver to the bowel. These vessels are the inferior vena cava, the portal vein and the hepatic artery. Clamps are placed on the vessels to stop blood flowing while your diseased liver is being removed. Your gallbladder is also removed. In some patients this reduction in blood returning to the heart puts a strain on the heart and in these situations an alternative must be found and a bypass is used. This means making another cut in your groin — generally on the right side. A tube is placed in the vein to transport the blood from the lower part of your body. A second tube is then placed in your abdomen to transport the blood from the liver and bowel. This blood passes through a machine and is returned to the heart via a line in your neck reducing the strain on your heart. Sounds so simple, doesn't it? This is not to be tried at home.

At this stage the surgeons now start to prepare the new donor liver for transplantation. Once this has been completed, they will remove your liver and your gallbladder and start transplanting the new liver. This involves joining your blood vessels to those of the donor liver. There are four joinings, otherwise known as anastomoses to be completed.

The vena cava above the liver.

9

The vena cava below the liver.

The portal vein.

The hepatic artery.

When these four joinings are completed the clamps on these are removed and your own blood starts to flow through the new liver. The surgeons then complete the remaining joinings. Once this part of the surgery is completed, and the surgeons ensure that there is no bleeding evident, they will insert two drains in your abdomen to monitor this and your wound will be closed. Staples or sutures are used to close the skin. Dressings will be placed on your wound and bags will be attached to the drains to collect any fluid that drains.

On average, patients lose between two and six litres of blood during the surgery. This is replaced as required as the surgery progresses. You will then be transferred back to your bed and will be taken to the Intensive Care Unit. You will be asleep for anything between 24 to 48 hours. A ventilator will be helping you to breathe and allow your body to rest. As an assigned nurse remains at your bedside, there will be drips hanging from nearly every part of your body. Those drips in your arms and neck enable your carers to administer the required fluids. You will have a catheter in your bladder to drain your urine and tubes up your nose, one of which will be used to feed you. The painkillers will be gradually reduced as soon as you are fully awake.

On June 24 I was admitted to Vincent's and underwent an MRI scan the following morning. This was followed by a session of chemotherapy, involving insertion through the groin. The hopes of that young doctor the previous January, that I would not need a transplant, had been dashed. The doctor who was about to administer the chemotherapy explained that he would be going right into the tumour and was hopeful of *"burning it away"*. Oh, God, I thought, another reprieve from a transplant.

But just as that thought was racing through my mind, he spoiled it all and seemed to know what I was thinking when he added, *"Of course you will still have to have a transplant, as you also have psoriasis of the liver."*

I had heard before of how sick one can be after a chemotherapy session, but I would never have imagined how bad it could be. I had endured plane, train, sea, food, and drink sickness in my day. Here I was having it all in one. That is what it felt like.

The summer of 2009 was one of the wettest in history, and for me it was one of the longest in my life. I had been told that I would have three hours to reach St Vincent's Hospital when or if a liver became available. Three hours might appear a reasonable period, but so much would depend on the time of the day or the day of the week when that call might come. I could imagine getting myself stuck in tea-time traffic or some other hold-up on the N4 or M50. I knew that a garda escort would be available to steer us on that 50-mile run, but I didn't want that kind of fuss. My brother Seamus had used a garda escort when his day arrived and he still talks of how brilliant the gardai were.

But being on the transplant waiting list also meant that you couldn't stray too far from your home. On several occasions while on short trips to places such as Tullamore, which is about 22 miles from my native Edenderry, there was always an uneasy feeling. What if I get the call now? Will I go straight to Dublin, or will I go home first? It was like living on an invisible *"death row"*. Of course what I was not aware of was that all the family, Eileen in particular, were experiencing the same stress. I didn't appreciate that at all. They hid their worries from me, and I suppose I tried to do likewise, keeping my concerns to myself. Eileen, who never takes chances, had my bags packed but even so, I was still thinking that when that call would come we'd probably all freak out and lose half-an-hour falling over ourselves trying to get my things together.

The preparation for transplant surgery is intense. They check you from your toes to your teeth and everything in between. On September 23 I attended St Vincent's to have two teeth extracted as part of that final preparation. This would be the final procedure before, hopefully, getting the transplant. My daughter Sinead brought me up on that occasion and I can remember, as we drove along the M50, discussing for the umpteenth time our strategy when the call would come. I checked into St Vincent's early that morning and had been fasting from 6am. The day wore on and there was no sign of my getting a bed. Eileen and Sinead observed that there was quite an amount of activity at the Nurse Station in St Brigid's Ward which is the Liver Unit. But we reckoned that was natural enough for this busy part of a great hospital. Nearing one o'clock a nurse came into us and said, *"That procedure might not be going ahead today. We'll have more news on that within the next hour."* I was absolutely starving. If the procedure was going to be cancelled that day, then the sooner the better, I thought. The fact that it might be cancelled made me even hungrier. Less than an hour later a second nurse appeared and told us that the procedure would not be going ahead.

Staring at me she continued, *"There might be another procedure in the morning."* We all looked at each other, and then it just dawned on me. I asked her bluntly, *"Are you talking transplant?"* Crossing two fingers on her right hand she replied, *"Hopefully. Doctors have been dispatched to check out a liver. We don't know yet, and we won't know until later on this evening."*

We didn't know whether to laugh or cry but I could see that Eileen and Sinead were thrilled. I was a little indifferent at first. Then, I thought, *"Well sure this is it. Isn't this what I've have been waiting for!"* Eileen was very positive as was Sinead with both of them pointing out that if the liver was for me then it was something of a miracle in that I was actually in the hospital when it became available. Looking back now, I suppose it was. Now I will never know how I would have reacted had I been at home when that call came. Eventually, the authorities at St Vincent's told us that we could go for something to eat. We made a beeline for the Dundrum Shopping Centre and I was content to settle for the Kentucky Fried Chicken outlet. I was very calm and remained so right up to the time of saying farewell to the family.

We returned to St Vincent's after 7pm and I was assigned a bed. It was getting closer, and I was getting a bit anxious, but hiding it as best I could. My two sons, Kevin and David, had left their respective places of employment and had arrived in Dublin. They were acting very normally, which was the correct thing to do in the circumstances. We were all in the waiting room at approximately 9.10pm when a nurse came in and announced what we all wanted to hear. *"The liver is suitable. You will be going down to theatre at 3.45am."*

Again, I had mixed emotions and I noticed that none of us looked at each other. No-one spoke. That just might have sparked off an emotional reaction that wouldn't have helped the situation. We went to the ward and I prepared to get into bed, while sending text messages to some friends asking them to pray. The replies were so positive, so reassuring and so much appreciated. I was back in the waiting room as the time ticked away, and finally I could see hospital personnel arriving and a porter with a wheelchair.

Now I was starting to get a bit anxious. This was definitely it. *Would I survive it? Would I ever see my family again? Was this the way that God has designed for me to go? Was I ready to meet him?* Jesus, was I sorry for all the sins. *Had I time to make amends, to repent? What would Eileen do now?* I knew it was major surgery. But my brother had been through it. He said he'd go through it again. All right for him to say that, I thought. He was now on the other side of it. *What if I don't wake up?* I thought that I'd better hold up for everyone's sake, including my own.

The porter wheeled me into the lift. We all crowded in. Still not a word spoken. He pressed the button and down we went. He opened the door of the lift and there we were just a few feet from the theatre door. It was time to say our farewells. It wasn't easy, and having an audience of hospital personnel standing around didn't make it any easier. This was the hardest part. We hugged. I held back the tears, but barely. The porter pushed the chair onwards and Eileen, Sinead, Kevin and David walked the other way. We were all gutted. I couldn't bear to turn around to see them walking away. I could hear their footsteps fading away. Within seconds I was in theatre and the anaesthetist was with me and telling me what was going to happen. I wasn't listening and I didn't want to hear anything he had to say. The next thing I remember was waking up in the Intensive Care Unit. Now that was a strange experience.

It was the strangest feeling I have ever encountered. I can remember seeing Kevin and David wearing what looked like plastic aprons and they were smiling over at me. But it appeared as if they were actually floating. I was trying to reach out to them, but I couldn't. I felt that we were in different worlds, different places. Maybe we were? Then they disappeared. The next thing I can remember was Eileen holding my hand and telling me the operation was over and it was a success. Again, I was doubtful if this was real or fantasy. It was then that I cried and cried and cried. I really broke down. I couldn't get it into my head that it was all over. I can remember asking the nurse at my bedside if the operation was over, and she assured me it was and that I was in the Intensive Care Unit and doing very well.

"You are fine, you are doing so well and they are delighted with you," she assured me.

I didn't enjoy being transferred from the ICU to the High Dependency Unit. I was very, very sore and while they were very gentle and extremely careful it hurt as they moved me from one bed to another. But they don't believe in letting pain linger on in St Vincent's and I must have near-emptied their drugs cabinet in the first few days.

Within a week I was moved to a ward and then the visitors started arriving. I was tired, I was sore, but I knew that I was one of the lucky ones. I realised that all the prayers had helped to give me a new lease of life. It was time to be thankful. It was important to continue praying that my body wouldn't reject the new liver. It was time also to think of the donor and the donor's family, and be forever grateful. A former colleague who had just retired from *The Star* through illness reminded me that I went to surgery on the feast of Saint Padre Pio.

Eileen never missed a day visiting me at St Vincent's, which wasn't easy. She wouldn't drive in city traffic, so she had to organise transport from home each morning and a way home each night. Thankfully, I have a great family, a great extended family, great neighbours, great friends and a community that always reaches out when the chips are down.

I arrived home from St Vincent's on October 16, but was re-admitted just three days later with a suspected infection of one of the wounds. However, I was discharged again on October 21. I came home to one of the worst winters in 50 years and I was confined to my sitting room couch for quite some time. Eileen had a full-time job carrying in turf and timber for the fire to keep me warm. Despite the frost I insisted on going out on St Stephen's Day for a short walk. Fifty yards would do. Just to see if there was any fresh air left. My son David came with me and just as we got outside the gate he warned me that the road was very icy and that I was to stay on the gravel area. He no sooner had the words out when my two feet went from under me and I landed on my rear end with my walking stick landing underneath me. What a fright! Thankfully David was with me and he helped me back up and back to the house. That ended my walking for weeks.

Towards the end of January I thought I was fit to venture out again. By now I was able to walk alone. Then one morning while out walking I felt very breathless. I decided to visit my GP, Dr Philip Brady who immediately ordered me to Tullamore Hospital. I had contracted pneumonia. I spent from Thursday, January 26 to Monday, February 1 there. I received no medication but was prescribed the necessary medication by my GP when I came home. I made a slow recovery and was just out of the woods at the end of March when I got the notorious winter vomiting bug. My God, this was something else. Had my GP told me that time that I had an hour to live it would have been such a relief. It lasted about five days, but the fall on December 26 set me back a long time.

As summer 2010 arrived I started staying out for longer periods, but the breathlessness remained and an X-ray revealed scarring of the lung caused by the pneumonia. It was a life-changing experience. There isn't one single day that I have not remembered or recounted some part of that experience, but there isn't one day that I don't thank God and pray for my doctors, donor, nurses, my wife Eileen who was with me 24/7 and my family and friends who carried me through it.

CHAPTER 2

Early Days

WHEN I was growing up in County Offaly, our house was on a sandy hill overlooking the vast expanse of Bord na Mona (BNM) bog named by the Bord as Glashabawn Works. They put Irish names on all their works. Our house was a BNM house built for employees and my father, being the first foreman appointed back in the late 1940s, qualified for the first house. He signed the rent agreement on April 1, 1950 for £32.10.0 per annum payable weekly at 12 shillings and sixpence to be paid each Friday in advance. He had started his career on the first bog developed by Bord Na Mona at Clonsast near Portarlington. He cycled the 25-mile round trip from Edenderry for 11 years before being appointed in charge of the new bog at Glashabawn. In Clonsast he had worked with the real pioneers of bog development, the legendary Gorman brothers, Pat, Joe and Dick.

We lived just over three miles from Edenderry and we walked to school regardless of the weather. There were no school buses and we didn't have a car. Many years later we got bikes. It was a long walk along a bleak road for children aged from just five years. Back then you wore short trousers in school until you were 10 or 12, so can you imagine the hardship of walking that distance in snow and rain and frost. Our first school was in an old building heated by turf-fuelled solid stoves. They were too warm if you had to sit near them but they were incapable of heating the entire classroom. The building was rat-infested and made national headlines one time when it was discovered that the rats were drinking the ink. Not alone were they drinking the ink they were able to remove the tiny ceramic inkwells from the desks. They were discovered underneath the floorboards. Unfortunately many boys were beaten silly before it was discovered it was the rats that were drinking the ink and removing the inkwells.

It was the era when corporal punishment was legally allowed in schools and was the norm. In my view, it was a brutal, terrifying regime. The teachers concerned have passed on but the memories remain. They used long canes purchased in the local Holts Hardware Shop.

They put electrical insulating tape on the end of the cane to prevent it from splitting and also to add more weight. They slapped you for not sitting straight, slapped you for not standing up straight, slapped you for laughing, slapped you for crying, slapped you if you suffered from a stammer, slapped you if you had a lisp or could not pronounce a word properly. Worse still, pupils with stammers or lisps were often ridiculed in front of the other pupils. Some teachers even slapped you for farting in class. But being slapped for being unable to learn was criminal, in my book. Discipline, I believe in, and perhaps it is now gone too far in the opposite direction, but to be flogged for being unable to learn is unthinkable. There were pupils who had dyslexia. Of course it hadn't been diagnosed back then. There were pupils who would be classed today as "special needs". The cure back then was to beat them stupid. This only made them worse.

Perhaps I should not speak ill of the dead. But I often wondered how we were so unfortunate to get such a gang of sadistic bastards in the same school at the same time. Then I put it down to the fact that the principal was a real brute and this probably gave the green light to the others to do the same. One teacher would catch you with his thumb and finger by the locks and lift you out of your desk. When you'd scream in agony he'd beat you with a cane. Our regime was similar to the one that existed in the nearby notorious borstal school in Daingean. The only difference I found was that we were allowed to go home in the evenings. When pupils reached the age of 14 in Edenderry the majority of them just walked across the road to work in the shoe factory. Some of them went home the first evening from there wondering how they got through a day without being slapped.

As I have said, the teachers who tormented us have all passed on. So what of the other teachers? We had Padraig *'Pee'* Flynn for a period. He was later to win fame as a TD for his native Mayo, a Government Minister and ultimately European Union Commissioner. A native of Castlebar, he often got me to post letters home to his Mum. I can vividly recall the address as being New Street, Castlebar.

Flynn was obsessed with the 17th century Irish hero Patrick Sarsfield. We learned his life story off by heart and particularly his renowned *"ride to Ballyneety"*, when Sarsfield's cavalry destroyed a convoy with a cannon bound for King William's troops, who were laying siege to Limerick in 1690.

For years I couldn't bear to go through the village of Lucan in County Dublin where there is a pub called the Sarsfield Bar. It brought those school days back to me. The first time I arrived in the Limerick village of Ballyneety I imagined Sarsfield riding this big white horse down the main street and *'Pee'* following up close behind.

On this particular day in class, Flynn was ranting on and on about Sarsfield and I had no interest. Instead, I found it much more enjoyable to play with a gear wheel or sprocket from an old alarm clock. I was spinning it on the desk, as children did back then. Real toys were scarce. Flynn looked down and caught me spinning my gear wheel and called me up for not paying attention. When I told him what I was doing he confiscated the gear wheel.

"Now I'll spin the wheel and you hold out both hands. I'm going to spring the wheel and I'm going to slap you until it stops," he said. By the time the gear wheel had stopped spinning Flynn had administered 22 slaps with his cane. I met an old school friend recently who recalled the incident and we reminisced about old times.

I started my schooling with the nuns and was with them until the end of third class infants. They were St John of God Sisters and they gave great service, but again young girls complained that some of them were sadistic. I do remember having a Sister Bronagh in third infants. She beat me every time she found me writing with my left hand, something that is very prevalent in our clan. She continued to beat me until I wrote, or tried to write, with my right hand and ended up leaving me in the position that I cannot write properly with either. Then there was Sister Euphrasia, who started the school band. She was an auld darling and I have very fond and happy memories of her. When I started school I had to wait in the evenings for my older sister to take me home. I waited in her class and they were a long way ahead of me. But they were learning a poem at the time and although I was just in baby infants I learned the words of the poem quicker than some of the students in that senior girls' class. My sister told the nun and I was brought up to the top of the class to recite it. I still remember the poem.

"Let the wealthy and great roll in splendour and state,

I envy them not, I declare it,
I eat my own lamb, my own chicken and ham,
I shear my own fleece and I wear it.
I have lawns, I have bowers,
I have fruit, I have flowers,
The lark is my morning alarmer,
So my jolly boys now, here's God speed the plough,
Long life and success to the farmer."

The reason why I could pick up the words of this poem ahead of much older pupils is probably because I liked poetry but mostly because it wasn't beaten into me with a cane. Even today when I have to return to my old national school to vote it brings it all back. When I step behind that timber partition and take the pencil in my hand to cast my vote I imagine a teacher is standing over me waiting, maybe hoping, that I'll make a mistake. School for us back then didn't end on Friday evening. No, we had to face the same teachers every Sunday. They held a 9.30am Mass for school children. They slapped you if you were absent, unless you were sick and this required a letter from your parent or guardian. Each class had their own pews in church and your teacher knelt behind you. If you spoke to the pupil beside you, you were slapped the following morning. Don't be caught laughing or you'll be flogged. Once a month you had to go to confession. That was held on a Saturday. For us it meant walking those three-plus miles to the church between 11am and 1pm. That was your Saturday ruined. Then on the following morning you had to fast. Not even a drink of water. We had to get up at 8am and leave the house at 8.30am for the 9.30am Mass. It lasted an hour, meaning we headed back home at 10.30am, reaching home and getting the first bite to eat at 11.30am. We did that from the age of seven or after receiving First Communion. The Mass back then was in Latin and we didn't know, or care, what was going on. Two of my children attended the same boy's school in Edenderry and we never encountered one single complaint.

****

It was much more difficult for a young boy living in a rural area to make pocket money. If you lived inside the town there was always the chance to pick up some odd jobs from some of the local business premises. There was the odd seasonal job with farmers but it was pure drudgery with little reward. When they would come to pay you they'd turn their back in case you might see what money they had, and they'd look at the few pence a dozen times before finally parting. They'd make you feel you were robbing the church sacristy box. That work would be sowing or picking potatoes, both back-breaking jobs but perhaps not a bad as *"catching"* turf in the bog. One man cut the sod and then he literally threw it at you. You grabbed that big wet heavy sloppy piece of muck and you laid it on a barrow to be wheeled out by a third person so that it could be laid out on the ground to dry. If you missed the sod or let it fall, too bad — the next one came directly after it.

Back then there were three old pennies to be redeemed for the return of mineral or soft drink bottles. I used scour the local landfill which was conveniently located on both sides of the public road near Edenderry. I had to walk through it to get to the town, so it was no big deal to have a search for a bottle. I would wash them at a fountain on Murphy Street and then take them to either Bowman's or Norman's shop and collect the pennies. I needed four bottles to make one shilling and my mother would give me the additional one penny so that I could go to the Savoy Cinema. The admission was one shilling and one penny.

By accident I found a new way of making money that led to

a scam and it worked for quite some time. I was about 14 at the time and a pupil at the Vocational School. I cannot recall exactly how it started but an older friend of mine was showing me a fox that he had just shot. He told me there was a bounty on foxes. I didn't know what he was talking about, but he explained that if I took the fox's tongue to the local Garda station and filled in a form the Government would post me out a postal order for a half-crown. That sum, to a youngster back then, was massive. He cut out the fox's tongue and I took it home. The next morning I presented myself at the Garda station which was just beside the Vocational School. I placed the paper bag on the counter and told the young garda what was in the bag and asked for the form to fill in. He just ran out past me and down the hallway. I could hear him throwing up in the toilet. I waited a good five minutes before he finally shouted up at me, *"Get that fucking thing out of there and throw it in the bin at the back of the station."* Eventually he was able to provide the form and he helped me fill it in and then all I had to do was wait for the postman.

The postal order arrived about two weeks later and I was so delighted that I got an idea. I knew that this particular garda was never going to look at a fox's tongue, so I would steal a piece of red meat from home, that would be a rare thing in our house in every sense of the word, and on some occasions a friend of mine who worked in a butcher's shop would provide me with a piece of waste meat. I would wrap it in brown paper but make sure it was leaking through the paper before reaching the station. I would keep it hidden just in case it was some of the other gardai who were dealing with the public. But if my man was on duty I wouldn't get any nearer than three yards of the front door when he'd shout, *"Don't bring that yoke in here. Dump it and come in then."* This was the way to do it. But my luck ran out and my scam was over when he was transferred. I bumped into him on the street some days before his departure. *"I suppose you'll cry when I'm gone,"* he said smartly.

"I sure will," I replied, and little did he realise I was being serious.

Times were hard and few people had much money. But our Aunt Nan in America was the saving grace on so many Christmas occasions. She had left Ireland at the age of 18 in 1929 and was now living outside New York. Married to a Longford man, she had two sons. Every Christmas she would send us a Christmas card with a dollar note in it. Jesus, Mary and Joseph, as my mother used say, a dollar to a child in '60s Ireland was a small fortune. It was worth seven shillings and six pence back then. It would have been a good day's pay for some. We idolised our Aunt Nan. Her youngest son Jimmy is now a leading lawyer in San Francisco and I was proud to be in court with him when he successfully defended Maze escaper Kevin Barry Artt who was fighting an extradition order from Britain.

****

When I was growing up in the '60s, Edenderry had showbands, ceili bands, brass bands, school bands, and ballad groups. As regards showbands, we had *The Houston* who were a Country and Western outfit fronted by the late Kevin Nolan, a marvelous ballad singer who also performed with local band leader Sean Norman. The latter musician ran the first ceili band to appear on *The Late Late Show*. The Houston were later fronted by the late Liam Gibson, a Dubliner from Inchicore who later went on to sing with Brian Coll, Philomena Begley and Brendan Shine. Liam collapsed and died while performing in Banagher. Johnny Scariff from Dublin was another fine front man with The Houston.

Then we had *The Agents Showband* fronted by the late Gary Street (real name Joe Conway). Born in England of County Mayo parents he enjoyed chart success with a number entitled *Flippity Flop* written by the late Michael Bryan, who died in a car crash while returning from a gig. Michael was a brother of Gaelic footballer Willie Bryan, the first Offaly man to lift the Sam Maguire in 1971, when the county won the All-Ireland football final. The Agents were mainly a pop outfit but they were very polished and very professional. Taken over by Release Records their old name was dropped and the legendary sports broadcaster Jimmy Magee came up with the new name, *The Fairways.* They had a great brass section including Danny Slevin on trombone. Danny is still involved in the business and has written some great songs including a recent Brendan Shine hit, *Grandad*, and that haunting ballad *The Curragh Wrens*, based on the sad tale of the women, mainly prostitutes, who were camp followers of the British Army and who lived a miserable life in huts amid the furze on the Curragh in the mid-1800s.

Going back over the years, Edenderry boasted a choir that was the first choir to broadcast *"live"* on RTE Radio or Radio Eireann, as it was known. Local woman Marie Tyrrell was the first female band leader in Ireland and fronted St Mary's Ceili Band in the '40s and '50s. She is still performing.

As I have already outlined, there was a young nun in the local Saint John of God convent for whom I had a huge regard, Sister Euphrasia, and she started a school band. I was the drummer boy. Another member of that band was Pauric Brown. Unlike me, he continued as a musician and carved out a very successful cabaret career and came second in the Irish version of Opportunity Knocks presented by Hughie Green in the mid-1970s. He enjoyed chart success with a song called *The Titanic* and at one stage was managed by the legendary Donie Cassidy. Sister Euphrasia was transferred to Kilkenny and I cried for weeks. I was her pet, and I loved her dearly. The band was taken over by Padraig *'Pee'* Flynn, and after a while it folded.

Edenderry is proud of having produced well-known personalities such as comedian Neil Delamere, singing priest Father Liam Lawton and RTE producer/researcher Cora Ennis. All three grew up just doors away from each other on St Mary's Road. Playwright Eugene O'Brien (Pure Mule, Savoy and Eden) is a proud Edenderry man, while fashion designer Geraldine Larkin works for the company that designed the outfit worn by Michelle Obama at the inauguration of her husband as US President. Ger Byrne, who played Malachy in the RTE soap Fair City, is also an Edenderry man. Greg Traynor, also from the town, is perhaps the best Elvis impersonator in the country and has done several TV adverts. In the sporting world the town has had representatives on the Offaly football and hurling teams, and has also been represented nationally in boxing, badminton, snooker and golf.

The East Offaly town can also boast of having had Sinead Flanagan as a teacher in the boys' school in the 1920s. She went on to marry Eamon de Valera, who became President of Ireland. As already outlined, *"Pee"* Flynn taught in the same school in the 1960s, and Terry Wogan, who went on to become one of the UK's leading broadcasting personalities, also has an Edenderry connection — he worked in the local branch of the Ulster Bank in the 1960s.

Although *"buried"* in the Bog of Allen, the Edenderry I grew up in had much more to offer than it has today. It had a cinema that changed movies five times a week. We had the Town Hall and Flanagan's Hall, two school assembly halls, 22 active sports clubs and good employment. The local Shoe Factory employed up to 500 people. It was run by Norman Watchman, a Jewish man, who was a good employer. Things were going so well in the '70s around Edenderry that the Shoe Factory and a textile factory named Group Textiles were forced to bus in workers from adjoining villages. Mangan's Coach Works, which secured Government contracts for the construction or adaption of various such vehicles had almost 300 employees and we had Corcoran's Engineering Ltd with another 100 workers. We had Bord na Mona, the ESB and a smaller private turf-harvesting company called the Shamrock Machine Turf Company. There was uproar in the '70s when it was discovered that the owner of the local Shoe Factory, Norman Watchman, had written to the IDA telling it that Edenderry did not require further industry as he was finding it hard to get enough workers to keep his factory going. God, how times have changed! The leaked letter was read at the AGM of Edenderry Fianna Fail Comhairle Ceantair where there were over 400 people present. Fianna Fail was huge in this area and they were led that time by the colourful TD, and Minister of State, Ger Connolly. Poll-topping Connolly was an expert at the old-style public meetings and he could rally his supporters with his quick wit. He is still remembered for his speech before a massive crowd in Tullamore's O'Connor Square during an election campaign. Highlighting FF's housing policy, he told the converted, *"I would like to tell all the young men here tonight in North Offaly and beyond, youse get the bird and we'll supply the cage."*

Our house was located beside the Glashabaun Bord na Mona (BNM) workshop and I spent many days and evenings there. I was messing around with dangerous equipment from the age of five but times were different and safety standards were not as stringent as today. I was lucky not to have lost a body part, and I got away with all kinds of devilment. Apart from that my father was the local foreman and the employees in and around the workshop wouldn't say anything to me. Some of them were very decent and you would get the odd penny, three penny bit or maybe sixpence from some fitters or electricians or ordinary workers. I remember the generosity of men like Martin Mullins, John Moynihan, Jimmy Touhy, "Bisto" Kelly, Joe Kelly, Tom Quirke, Bill Gantley, Johnny Doyle and many more.

The huge locomotives that pulled thousands of tonnes of turf from the bogs to the tip head for loading onto lorries as well as into the Power Station at Allenwood were always parked in the yard next to our yard. They were massive machines with massive engines. I was so young that I would have to grip the gear handle with my two hands to pull it into gear. It had three forward gears and a reverse. When everyone had gone home and my father was away working on our small holding a half a mile from the house, I would start up the loco and move it a few feet. Then eventually I got brazen and confident and I'd take it for a spin.

I can vividly recall a Sunday afternoon when a businessman from Edenderry arrived out to the BNM workshop with his young children. I asked if they would like a trip out the bog on a loco. The businessman obviously saw nothing wrong with this and he agreed. I gave them a very enjoyable trip. So I could say that I was way ahead of BNM themselves in organising bog trips. I was 11 years of age at the time.

My father died from lung cancer on July 27, 1959, two days after his 47th birthday, leaving my mother with ten young children, a few cows and calves and two small holdings inherited from his father. The land was mainly bog and it wouldn't sustain snipe, never mind a family of eleven. My father had worked for BNM for almost 26 years, but he was hardly 26 days dead when they sent their officials to tell us that they wanted their house vacated forthwith. I can remember his funeral. There was a big crowd. All the Bord na Mona works were closed down for the day as a mark of respect. His death didn't affect me that much...at the time. One of my favourite BNM employees,

Christy *"Bisto"* Kelly from Rathangan, who attended the funeral, gave me two half-crowns. Jesus! The Lotto! And then he gave me a ride down town on his 750cc Sunbeam motorcycle, registration number XML 176. We eventually got a stay put on BNM's eviction order thanks to the intervention at the time by the local Parish Priest, Monsignor Martin Brennan, and we built our own house, forcing my mother to sell off the livestock.

From our BNM house you could look across the vast BNM bogs that stretched for miles. It was a cross between the Sahara and the Everglades. In the summer you couldn't see for dust while in winter you'd find it hard to walk on the soft, boggy surface. But now that it has been drained it is much dryer, but of course prone to flooding in the winter. Back then in those glorious summer days you could gaze from our yard at the people footing the turf. *"Footing turf"* means arranging the sods so that the wind and sun can dry them as quickly as possible. The BNM turf-cutting machines delivered a sod of turf that was shaped like a gold bar, only much bigger. It measured 15 inches in length, four inches wide and approximately three inches thick. After a week on the ground it is about ready to *'foot'.* This meant turning over the sods and laying two more on top of them at right angles. You continued that pattern until you used 10 sods and you ended up with a hollow cube shape approximately 20 inches high. In other parts of the country, particularly the west of Ireland, four sods would be stood on end, leaning against each other, to speed the drying process. Looking out at the turf-footing from our house was a sea of colour with as many women as men footing. Men didn't like footing turf, particularly the culchies. They felt it was a woman's job, and women were indeed very good at it. When I say *"culchies"* I mean mostly the people who arrived from the West of Ireland. The word *"culchie"* is derived from the town of Kiltimagh in Mayo.

Some young lads loved footing directly behind the women because back then women didn't wear slacks or trousers or jeans. So when a gush of wind came it would lift their dresses and some lads would see maybe even more than they bargained for. I remember one guy telling me, *"Jaysus I was behind an auld wan today from Ticknevin. Her dress blew up with the wind. Oh, my gawd. She had big blue double gusset knickers and you could dip bread between her legs."* It certainly put me off dip bread for a long time. I hated bog work as did most of my brothers. I remember my late brother Liam arguing with my mother over having to go to work in our own bog to harvest our own winter fuel.

"How come the people who live in Dublin don't have to go to the bog," he'd say.

"Ah, but I bet they'd love to have a bog to go to," replied my mother.

"Well, they can have ours," said Liam.

Of course Edenderry opened its doors to many people from so many counties and countries as far back as the late '40s with the advent of Bord na Mona. Vast bogs were being developed and there was a famine for workers, or slaves. Men arrived from all over Ireland and I wouldn't underestimate their difficulties on arrival. They were housed in purpose-built hostels, each hostel made up of several billets with each billet accommodating between 24 and 32 men.

They were cold concrete buildings and the beds resembled something from a German concentration camp. Indeed, the entire set-up and system resembled something from a German concentration camp. One BNM worker once described the camps as *"a place or state of punishment where the culchie suffers before taking the Mail Boat to England".*

The men who arrived in the early years to work on the development of the bogs were treated virtually like slaves. The work was hard, the pay was poor and the accommodation was atrocious. Camps built by Bord na Mona around the bogs included one at The Derries near enderry and one in Killinthomas, near Rathangan. The roofs were made of asbestos. The walls were concrete, they were heated by pot-belly stoves and were sparsely furnished. The wardrobes were made of plywood and those erected near the stoves warped with the heat.

The food was terrible. John Hayes, who still lives in Rathangan, came to the BNM Works at Boora in West Offaly in 1951 from Kilfinane, County Limerick. From there he went to Mount Dillon in Roscommon before moving to The Derries near Edenderry and finally to Killinthomas, Rathangan. John said that the breakfast was okay. They were served rashers, sausages, eggs and black and white pudding. But he added that the black pudding was so hard you could use it to make bullets. *"The lunch you got going out on the bog was really something else. You'd get a half a loaf of bread with a lump of butter stuck to the side of it and a few ounces of tea. You never had enough tea and had to subsidise the ration. But the bread was dreadful."* John explained that the beds had a solid base and they covered that base with three cushions or *"biscuits"* as they were known by all the employees. They were given six army blankets and the cost per week for board and lodgings was £1. He says that when BNM were recruiting they arranged for workers to pick up a travel voucher from their local Labour Exchange. This entitled you to travel by train or bus to Dublin or whatever location you required. According to John Hayes, a lot of Kerrymen availed of the voucher and took the train to Dublin and the bus to Aston Quay. This was vouched for. But when they reached Aston Quay they took a bus to Dun Laoghaire then jumped on the Mail Boat to Holyhead. Goodbye Eire and thanks a lot, Bord na Mona.

Larry Costello, who also lives in Rathangan, came to work

at Glashabawn Works three miles from Edenderry at the tender age of 20. He admits to being very, very lonely. He had left his native Fuerty in Roscommon and travelled on the CIE bus to Edenderry with two other pals from his own area. But they were separated at the bus stop and Larry was sent alone to The Derries camp. He recalled the primitive accommodation. *"If the rats didn't eat you the fleas would,"* he said. Larry said that the army blankets handed out were too light, like bee's wings. He was handed a shovel and ordered to dig drains. Dig, dig, dig, was the order of the day. But if that was hard, he maintains that working on the very first German turf-cutting machines was pure slavery. They also wheeled turf out on barrows and according to Larry one would sink to their knees while wheeling them. Then the Bord invented a strap that reached from the handles of the barrow up and around your neck. He also criticised the lunch given to them each morning and said that the beef served for dinner was like leather. He later moved to Killinthomas Camp in Kildare, where he was to meet a young girl by the name of Mary Kennedy, who worked in the kitchen. They married and are still living happily just outside the County Kildare village. Larry got several invitations to join family members who emigrated to England but he opted to stay at home. While he still says the work in BNM was pure slavery he is glad he remained in Ireland.

But it wasn't all culchies who inhabited the camps. Albert Reynolds, who went on to become Taoiseach, stayed at Killinthomas Camp when he worked as a wages clerk in Ballydermot Works from June 1952 until April 1953, and his works number was 5345. The wages were small and former employees recall Albert footing turf in the evenings to supplement his wages. Albert was fond of the horses and each Saturday when the Curragh Races were on he would ride the ten-mile journey from Rathangan on his bicycle to the racecourse.

BNM employees worked long hours digging drains in near swamp-like conditions on piece rate. That means they got paid by the yard or the metre. If the drain you dug caved in overnight, then you didn't get paid until you did it all over again. Then came the giant turf-cutting machines called *"Baggers"*. They weighed hundreds or thousands of tonnes and it was rather difficult keeping them from sinking in the marshy-type ground. Men working on the *"baggers"* worked shifts including 12 midnight to 8am and they were forced to wear hip boots. They were badly treated by their employers and on one occasion when they went on strike for better conditions, Bord na Mona heads in Dublin, most of whom had probably never worked or perhaps never even seen a bog, ordered that the water be cut off. They left the workers without a drink. Local Councillor Jim Flanagan marched the workers, 5,000-strong, into Edenderry's O'Connell Square. He then approached the town's leading businessman, Eugene J.P. O'Brien, and ordered him to bake enough bread in his bakery to feed the starving men. He ordered meat from a local butcher and he fed the hungry through a window in his own house at St Francis Street. Councillor Flanagan once showed me cheques issued by BNM to workers during and after the strike — in the sum of one penny.

The camps were equipped with canteens. There was what was known as *"wet"* and *"dry"* canteens. The names speak for themselves and the culchies spent most of their time in the wet canteens. They were young men who had arrived from all over Ireland. They were lonely and away from home for the first time. Perhaps that is why they drank so much. They also had a recreation hall where they held dances and staged concerts. I have a vague memory of being taken to a concert. I can just remember seeing the curtain on the stage being pulled across.

They also had a sports field and they held annual sports days.

I have vivid memories of walking to school through Murphy Street, or as it was locally known the *"Tunnel Road"*. This road led from the town to a Bord na Mona hostel at The Derries, the area where I was born and raised. There were at least nine counties represented on this one street alone. These were men who had come to work in the bogs, married locally and got houses, or stayed with families instead of staying in the flea-ridden and rat-infested hostels. Edenderry became their adopted town and some of them were among its finest citizens. I can recall with fond memories men like Jim McMenamin and Willie Grehan (Mayo), Joe Reilly (Longford), Jack Hutchinson (Waterford), Tommy Smith (Cavan), Ned Gately, (Roscommon), John Ryan, (Tipperary), Joe Enright (Limerick), Jim Byrne (Wexford), Johnny Keogh (Cork), and the local shopkeeper Andy Bowman from Waterford. Although Andy was not connected in any way with Bord na Mona, he provided a fine service to those who were.

I have always maintained that the phrase *"How's she cutting?"* was first coined in the Bord na Mona bogs. In the early '50s the huge-turf cutting machines were equipped with short-wave radios. They had quite a radius and I have fond memories of sneaking into the workshop beside our house in the evenings. I would switch on the radio and talk and sometimes sing to all the machines operators across the entire Glashabawn and Ballydermot bogs. Sometimes I would be asked by workers going on shift at 4pm to check racing results and give them a call. I remember one particular machine driver by the name of Tom Quirke, a Wexford man, requesting that I listen in to an athletic event on Radio Eireann from Melbourne. It involved some athlete called Herb Elliott. I was only eight years old at the time. Thankfully, my father never found out about my radio escapades.

The turf-cutting machines worked 24/7 and during those long, lonely nights on barren bogs the workers would decide to call the nearest machine just for company. They had little in common and in most cases mightn't even know each other as they could even be staying in different hostels or camps. So the most common opener would be *"How's she cutting?"* meaning how is the bagger cutting the turf. They weren't really interested in whether she was cutting or sunk to the bottom of the trench, but it was a good line for openers.

A lot of the men who came to work on the bogs used it as a means of making a few pounds that would take them to England plus a few bob in their pockets to get them by until they got a job with McAlpine, Wimpy or John Lang. When those ex-BNM workers would meet on city streets, or in any of the hovels where they drank, they would nearly always greet each other with the words, *"How's she cutting?"*

But the huge influx of men from around the country brought its problems. Many of the men had nothing to do after hours but drink. The men, always referred to by the locals as *"culchies"*, were not too popular with local men, as local women were warming to the strangers, who were seen by the local males as love rivals and a threat. It resulted in running battles and at times Edenderry resembled Dodge City without the guns. Something had to be done to restore law and order and while no new legislation was enacted the powers-that-be sent in what they thought was the answer in Garda Sergeant Martin O'Neill. He ruled with a baton and administered summary justice. He left many a culchie with a sore skull.

A District Court case of that time revealed how a large number of men from a BNM camp laid siege to the local Garda station after one of their colleagues was arrested by Sergeant O'Neill.

The case as published by *The Irish Times* reads:

"A baton charge and other incidents were described at Edenderry District Court by Civic Guard Sergeant M. O'Neill when charges of riotous and disorderly conduct were preferred against Patrick and Stephen Connolly (brothers), Castlegar, Co. Galway; Patrick Coleman, Hollymount, Co. Mayo, and Michael Duffy, Dereendufderry, Killawalla, Co. Mayo.

"The sergeant said he was passing Coleman and the others on the street, when Coleman made loud noises with his mouth and he (witness) turned back and asked him for his name. He refused to give it and the witness was taking him to the barrack when the others attacked him.

"The witness used his baton and in the struggle knocked Duffy unconscious with it. He was trying to get Duffy to the barrack when he tripped over a man lying behind him, and he was attacked on the ground by Coleman and the other defendants. A civilian came to his assistance, and Guards arrived and brought Coleman to the barrack. Duffy escaped, and had wandered around the country that night trying to get back to the Shean Turf Camp, which he reached at 3am. Both he and Coleman were brought to Newbridge Hospital for treatment, and were detained for some time.

"The District Justice fined these defendants 40 shillings to be paid within 14 days, or they would go to jail for one month. He allowed 20 shillings costs.

"The sergeant then related how, at midnight of the same night, about 100 men came from the turf camp and stood outside the barrack, shouting for Coleman's release. They began throwing stones, and broke two panes of glass in a window. The witness ordered a baton charge, and the Guards rushed at the men, while Detective Officer Reid fired shots over their heads from a revolver.

"The witness caught one man named Michael Carroll, a native of Clonmel, and struck him with his baton. The rest ran back to the camp. These incidents took place after midnight, after the

town lights were switched off, and in the dark stones were thrown, which injured Guard Ryan on the knee. Knives, cudgels and iron bars were found on the road by the Guards after the men had ran away.

"*The District Justice said he had received a letter from Carroll from Galway, where he was now employed. He was fined 20 shillings with 20 shillings costs, or in default, 14 days' imprisonment.*" I saw Sergeant O'Neill in action on one occasion and once was enough. He was a savage.

CHAPTER 3

From Hardware
To Show Business

IT IS not a nice feeling to be standing close to the doors of a dance hall with very little in your pocket and a band about to ask you for payment for their night's work. I was still just a teenager and working in a hardware shop in my native Edenderry when I decided to branch out into organising dances. I was little more than 16 years old when I began serving my time to the retail hardware trade in the UP Stores in my home town. It was one of the biggest hardware shops in the country and by far the biggest in the Midlands.

I knew from day one that I wasn't going to spend my life behind a counter, but the experience was great. I loved meeting people and in this establishment I believe I met them from all walks of life. The hardware trade back then was so different. It was harder too. Everything now comes packaged. In my day most things like nails, screws and staples were loose. You had to fill them by hand, winter and summer. I dreaded the farmers because they always came in around January and February looking for plough points. I hadn't a clue about plough points, other than they were fitted to a horse-drawn plough, they were pointed and they cut through the soil and shaped the drills. They were thrown on top of each other in the store and they were all different makes, sizes and shapes. You would be down on your knees in a badly lit and freezing cold store, and the rats running around you, looking for a particular plough point. Then when you found it they wanted it for half the marked price.

But they were no worse than women looking for wallpaper. It took me a long time to realise that the more patterns you showed them the harder they found it to choose one. Eventually I used show them only one or two pattern books. Then you had to show them borders to go with it, and like the farmer they wanted it for half nothing. But times were hard and money was scarce. If you didn't create your own fun in this job you'd crack up. I got great fun out of setting alarm clocks to go off in a customer's bag on their way home. Back then the women from Carbury, and particularly from a tiny townsland called Ticknevin would arrive in to Edenderry on the 3.15pm bus. It departed at 4.20pm so they had limited time to shop. All I can ever remember the women from Ticknevin buying were alarm clocks. When I had established that they were on the bus, I would set the alarm to go off about ten minutes into their journey. Everyone on the bus would know they had bought an alarm clock.

I was a bad time-keeper simply because I had little interest in the job and on the one morning I made it on time, the manager Joe Murrin looked at his watch as I came through the door. Then he looked at me, looked at his watch again and walked towards me. I was delighted. Here he was on his way to congratulate me on being on time. *"Were you locked in all night?"* he said and walked away.

I remember another day that all hell broke loose when one of the Bord na Mona (BNM) installations at

Ballydermot near Rathangan in Kildare phoned to say that something terrible had just happened to their lawn. Their beautiful manicured green lawn had suddenly turned brown. They said they had purchased fertiliser from our store for the lawn the previous week and there must have been something wrong with the product. Dockets were checked and it was discovered that I was the person who had served them. I was never big on science and it just struck me that instead of filling them a bag of sulphate of ammonia I had filled them a bag of sodium chlorate. Sort of sounded the same to me, but it wasn't the same. Sodium chlorate is a weed-killer. It was taken off the market in the '70s when it was discovered that the Provisional IRA were using it to make milk churn bombs. It was banned all across Europe from September 2009.

On the day of the BNM complaint I immediately filled a bag of sulphate of ammonia, wrapped it in brown paper, as I would or should have done the first day. Then I pulled it around a bit to make it look shabby, wrote BNM on the bag, and left it at the end of the counter. When the investigation was in full swing, I produced the bag from the end of the counter and said that the person who picked up the bag for BNM must have picked up the wrong one in error. It worked.

In October 1967, having enjoyed some good successes as a promoter of dances, I bade farewell to the hardware trade and hung up my brown shop coat. My vacancy was filled by a young lad from nearby Rhode. He even took my coat, and he was welcome to it. That young chap was Seamus Darby, who was destined to go down in Irish sporting history, and our paths were to cross again a decade or so later.

****

Growing up, like thousands of others, I was influenced by the emergence of the renowned ballad group, the *Clancy Brothers* and Tommy Makem and then of course by *The Dubliners*, fronted by the gravel-voiced Ronnie Drew. I hadn't much interest in showbands but all that changed one day when my immediate boss in UP Stores, the late Ernie Lawless, asked me to help him get home his turf from the local bog. It was a Thursday and that was the traditional half-day in our town. He took me to his home for lunch and I was aware that Ernie's sister Mary was going out with showband singer Larry Cunningham. The Longford man had hit the big time with his recording of *A Tribute To Jim Reeves* the previous year. Larry was to become one of the biggest attractions on the Irish ballroom circuit. While I wasn't into showbands back then I was excited when we arrived at Ernie's house to see Cunningham's pale blue Longford-registered Ford Cortina parked outside. There was no sign of Larry when we entered the house but I soon established that he had stayed over and was just getting out of bed. He was introduced to me and I can still remember how modest he was. He was pressed to sing a song for me and I became embarrassed. As young as I was I appreciated that it was very difficult for a man of his calibre to deliver a performance in someone's kitchen five minutes after getting out of bed without any musical backing. But Larry obliged and lifting one foot onto a kitchen chair he announced, *"This is an auld song we have just recorded and hopefully it might do well. It's the B-side of our next single. It's an auld song called Lovely Laytrom."* Well that auld song, *Lovely Leitrim*, was by popular demand turned into the A-side, and today very few would be able to tell you what the original intended A-side was. For the record (no pun intended) it was a number entitled *There's that Smile Again*. Well *Laytrom*, as Larry pronounced it, stayed in the Irish charts for 26 consecutive weeks. It became one of the most requested songs ever on RTE Radio and turned Larry Cunningham into a pop idol for young and old. I became friends with Larry, a friendship that remains to this very day. He brought me all over Ireland and I soon became a fan of the Irish showband scene and knew I wouldn't be happy until I dabbled in it myself.

I could not have been influenced by a better man. He chalked-up some many 'firsts' in his day and never allowed success or fame to affect him. There was no 'big head' with Larry and he personally abhorred anyone who was like that. I recall an occasion when someone asked him if he thought a certain Dublin-based singer would do a charity gig down the country. Larry clearly reckoned the guy would need plenty of publicity and recognition for his act of charity, and replied, *"Ah, he would surely, if you escorted him from around Lucan with the Artane Boys Band."* Larry's total lack of pretentiousness was what I admired most about him.

Larry was the first Irish singer to enter the British charts when *Tributes to Jim Reeves* came in at number 27. As far as I can recall he was the first showband singer to release an LP. It was titled *The Two Sides of Larry.* He became absolutely massive on the ballroom and marquee circuit and at one stage it was considered that none of the other big outfits on the circuit, like Joe Dolan, Brendan Bowyer, Dickie Rock or Butch Moore, would play within a 30-mile radius of Cunningham simply because he would wipe them out. He went on to draw massive crowds, from his native Granard to The Grand Ole Opry, and from Longford to London. In March 1966 he broke a 12-year attendance record held by the great Scottish entertainer Jimmy Shand when, fronting the *Mighty Avons*, he packed 6,800 punters into the famous Galtymore Ballroom in London's Cricklewood. While it looked well on the Mighty Avons' CV at the time there was a big down side to it, as the contract had been signed before Larry made the big breakthrough and they were playing on the night for a straight fee of £250 sterling. Larry lamented after the gig, *"If this fella wants me back he'll pay for me."*

Larry was a very shrewd operator. I can recall two incidents with Larry and the Avons that to me were hilarious at the time. On one occasion the lads in the band were going through a suit pattern book. That is how it was done back then and a famous operator in the rag trade was Jas Fagan in Dublin. He was as popular back then as Louis Copeland is now. The boys were studying the various shades and discussing the various *'cuts'* when they noticed that Larry, who was engaged in conversation with someone else, was not taking part in the exercise. Suddenly, one of the Avons, called, *"Hey Larry, will you have a look at this pattern book?"* Larry replied: *"Ah go ahead and pick out something 'daycent' and not too gawdy and make sure it's a suit we can wear to Mass when we're finished wearing it on stage."* It may have sounded comical but Larry was deadly serious.

The second such occasion was in Lawlor's Ballroom in Naas and it was the Avons' first gig after coming back from a tour of the United States. Apparently Larry's saxophone had become damaged on the flight and the lads were hoping that Larry had made the trip from his home in Granard to Dublin that day to get the saxophone repaired. As soon as Larry came through the dressing room door they all asked if he had made the trip to Dublin and was the sax repaired.

"I did in me arse make Dublin. When I eventually got up today I was that knackered I was hardly able to dress meself."

"Oh mother of fuck," said one of the band members. *"What are we going to do for a sax?"*

Grinning broadly, Larry said, *"There'll be not be a bother on it. I straightened it on me knee."*

The Mighty Avons had a manager at that time by the name of Charlie McBreen. As far as I can remember the late Charlie was from Omagh. He wasn't the brightest when it came to reading or writing, but he had it in abundance in other ways. He had a fantastic memory. If you asked Charlie in the month of February about a date for the following November, he'd scratch his head for a few seconds and say, *"Sorry sir, we're in Ballina that night."* He wouldn't be bluffing either. On one occasion when told by a festival committee that the official attendance was 1,942, he retorted immediately, *"That's one less than last year, sir. Who died?"*

Charlie arrived at a ballroom one day where the Avons were rehearsing. It was either the Granada in Cavan or the Granada in Granard. As he came through the door he was greeted by a row between two members. When he asked what the row was about he was told the lads were fighting over chords. *"Ah, for fuck's sake sir, aren't they earning enough money now to buy new ones?"* he replied.

On another occasion the band got lost in a blizzard on the way home from a gig in some part of rural Ireland. When the driver of the coach noticed a nameplate as they entered some village, he braked and asked Charlie to get out and see what was on the sign. Charlie obliged and walked back to the sign wiping off the snow with his sleeve. However, on his return he said he wasn't sure. He claimed he couldn't see it clearly. When pushed he said it was a place called *'Goslow'.* Failing to find such a village on their map, another member of the band got out to check and discovered that the sign read, *'Go Slow'*! On another occasion Charlie arrived at the office of a record company wondering what kind of "loyalties" might be due on the sale of a particular record. When commenting on the success or lack of success of a particular record McBreen is credited with saying, *"It would have gone better sir, only it didn't get the radio exposure."*

****

In Edenderry, local councillor Jim Flanagan had re-opened his ballroom, which had been closed for years and because of my new-found interest in showbands I ended up helping him get it ready. It was known in the 1940s and '50s as Flanagan's Hall and now it was about to be renamed the Eden Ballroom. I was given the prestigious task of painting the ceiling. The only resemblance between me and Michelangelo was the length of time it took me to do the job — it was a huge area.

The ballroom was massive. It re-opened in November 1966 for the local Edenderry Shoe Factory annual dance and the band on stage that night was *Tony And The Graduates*. They were, as we would term them back then, a "middle of the road" outfit, but capable of drawing a crowd, especially in Edenderry where they had never performed. But with up to 500 people working in the Shoe Factory it was probably a waste of money hiring a band of that calibre. You had a guaranteed crowd no matter who was playing. There was a local outfit, *The Houston Showband* whose members, well nearly all of them, were Shoe Factory employees. They would have sufficed. The ballroom was, as I said, absolutely massive and had been popular in the '40s and '50s and built by Jim Flanagan with his own hands, including the laying of a Canadian maple sprung dance floor that was the talk of the country. Other aspects of the hall were also spoken of for the wrong reasons. Jim refused to hang doors on the cubicles in the men's toilets. This ensured that they weren't used. Legally, he was complying with all the planning regulations.

A Dublin native, Jim ended up in Edenderry by accident, literally. Passing through the east Offaly town in the 1930s, Jim, a young engineer, came off his motorcycle at Kishawanny Bridge and was taken to the local Cottage Hospital. A young woman named Anna Kane worked there and they fell in love and married. Jim was a Labour supporter and played in the Irish Transport and General Workers Union (ITGWU) Fife and Drum band. He was close to the legendary trade union leader, Big Jim Larkin, and had the honour of attending meetings with him and driving him around the city in Larkin's final days. A very forceful councillor, Jim was also stubborn nd could be very single-minded. Once he got something into his head it would take brain surgery to change it. Like the time he was told that the big showbands were now demanding 60 per cent of the gross receipts. As far as he was concerned, they could have a running jump for themselves. He wasn't going to spend his time, money and sweat building a ballroom to give it all away to a shower of yahoos with long hair pulling desperately on guitar strings and creating noise that would frighten the Banshee. *"Who do they think they are with their tuppence ha'penny ukuleles?"* he once said.

Jim Flanagan had no time for religion and once made headlines following a meeting of the Edenderry Town Commissioners when he was asked during the meeting if he believed in Lourdes. The religious centre in France had become very popular with Irish pilgrims over the years, and dozens of miraculous cures were reported after people prayed at the grotto where Our Lady was said to have appeared in the 1850s. *"I will believe in Lourdes when I see some guy going with one leg and coming back with two,"* he replied.

Back then people were extremely loyal to their church and

their clergy, and Jim was soon branded a communist. Despite this, his popularity as a politician soared because he was prepared to fight for his people and stand up to authority. Physically he had no fears either, and would take on any man of any size, armed or unarmed, as he often did in his ballroom days. He was a trained wrestler and toured the world with the famous professional wrestler and legend Steve *'Crusher'* Casey and his wrestling brothers from Sneem in County Kerry.

In 1955 Jim was poised to head the poll in the Edenderry Town Commission election as a Labour candidate and so he decided to add on a few running mates. The Fianna Fail and Fine Gael candidates, most of them outgoing, panicked, and asked Jim to withdraw his running mates. Flanagan refused and hours before the nominations closed the candidates all assembled at the Town Hall in a final bid to persuade Jim to withdraw his two candidates. They made Jim an offer whereby all outgoing councillors would return en bloc.

Jim still refused and held firm. The FF and FG councillors walked into the Town Hall and withdrew their nominations and told Jim that there would be no election. As they argued outside with Flanagan and between themselves, Flanagan kept a close eye on the clock and when it struck 9pm he approached the then Town Clerk, Molly Earley and told her to declare himself and his two running mates elected. All hell broke loose and even High Court actions were threatened, but Flanagan, who was always a step ahead of the opposition, went off smiling. The following week he co-opted two more friends and they held power for five years.

Cllr Flanagan became very irate with members of Offaly County Council and officials sometime in the early 1970s when he was ousted from all the various committees following the council's annual general meeting. When the next meeting was held Jim was armed with a dozen hen eggs and he pelted the top table destroying the lovely pinstripe suits and the walls of the chamber, before the Gardai were called. When he ran out of eggs he grabbed a steel ashtray and let it off. It barely missed the chairman's head and crashed into the wall, taking out a huge piece of plaster. The mark was there for years before it disappeared during renovation. Had it struck anyone, serious injuries, or worse, might have resulted.

Jim had a running two-year battle with the Irish Parachute Club when they commenced operations near his home at Esker outside Edenderry and not far from the town of Daingean. To this day few, if any, know his real reasons for objecting. He always referred to them as *"cowboys"*, a title that they certainly didn't deserve. He claimed the parachutists were dropping into people's gardens and onto roads, in front of cars. He tipped me off as a journalist one Monday morning back in the early 1980s that sparks would fly at an Offaly County Council meeting that afternoon. As the meeting opened and the chairman had recited the opening prayer, Jim didn't disappoint and to the annoyance and utter disgust of members and officials he was on his feet shouting, *"These cowboys must be removed from operating at Esker."* Then he added, *"If any of these bastards ever land on my property they'll wish their parachute never opened."*

He went on to claim he had been told that a son of Fianna Fail leader Charles Haughey had also been parachuting, and he should be doing it on Charlie's own land up in Dublin, and he branded Charlie a "cowboy" in the process. This was before tribunals highlighted the massive payments from wealthy friends that were trousered by Charlie. The Fianna Fail members stormed out and the meeting was adjourned for almost an hour until things had calmed.

Jim Flanagan may have been a forceful councillor, he may

have dedicated his political talents to helping the less fortunate in society, and died nearly penniless as a result, but when it came to running a dance hall he hadn't got it. The hall ceased to operate as a ballroom, and it was sad to see it closing. It became a venue for Gael Linn bingo sessions, with guest appearances by noted sports broadcaster Jimmy Magee. Jim Flanagan was so stubborn that he'd burn it before giving it to someone else to run. If he couldn't run it then no-one else was going to run it.

As the 1970s approached, dance halls were closing fast, and just before they did my friend Michael Nolan and I approached Jim Flanagan for the use of his hall for a gig. Jim agreed to the letting, but did us no favours when it came to the fee. He took 40 per cent of the gross receipts and left us to pay for the band and the advertising from our 60 per cent. We booked a Cork-based band, *Pat Lynch And The Airchords*. The band were enjoying chart success with a song called *Irish Soldier Laddie*, which featured bagpipes and a great, versatile artist, Arthur O'Neill. I was nervous as the day drew close and there appeared to be very little talk about the gig. We asked our friends who owned cars to park them outside the hall. This was an old trick back then to give those arriving at the venue the impression that things were moving. It had a great effect. I had the equivalent of 11c in my pocket and the band was costing us the equivalent of €160. Early in the night someone had called in selling raffle tickets and I bought one, leaving me with small coins. I prayed like never before. My prayers were answered and as the pubs closed the crowd swelled with a total of 432 paying in. We made a few quid on that first venture and I was sure this was the way to go. Why spend a full week behind a hardware counter for approximately €5 a week when I could make €50 in three hours while listening to music and watching people dance!

But some months later when I booked another venue in

another county, Jim Flanagan was furious and accused me of using his hall as a stepping stone for other promotions. That is one example of how difficult he could be. So that ended our promotions at Flanagan's Hall or The Eden Ballroom. A small number of apartments now stand on the site and I'm glad that the apartments are officially named Flanagan Court. Jim and I ended up very close friends, and he was particularly good to me on an occasion when I was at rock bottom. I'm delighted and proud that I contacted the *Guinness Book of Records*, and had Jim officially recognised as the Longest Serving Politician in the World after serving for over 53 years. I still have the certificate issued by the Guinness Record Book.

The other venue I was now operating was a tiny hall in a place called Milltown on the edge of the Curragh and not far from Newbridge town. It was a small rural hall, but my philosophy was always that I'd prefer to have a small hall full than a big one half-empty. It was all down to psychology, and we are, after all, a simple race. The capacity of the hall was around 200 and how we managed to squeeze almost 700 into it one night is still a mystery. I think the law stated that you had to provide six square feet per person. Had that law been strictly enforced the dance hall days would have ended much sooner.

For my first gig in Milltown I booked a solo singer named Danny Doyle and I was using a small band that I had just become acquainted with called *The Concords*. Danny Doyle was booked and confirmed for €37.97 (£30) and just weeks before he was due to appear, he shot to number one in the Irish Charts with a popular ballad called *Whiskey On A Sunday*. He was the rave of the country and I was rubbing my hands in delight. Then his management contacted me trying to cancel the date or get more money for him. He was now securing €379 (£300) for engagements but I had no intention of adding a nought to my agreed fee. I stood my ground and said that I had everything in writing. Danny Doyle drew a massive crowd and apart from an almighty row, to which the Kildare gardai had to be called, it was a great night. I paid The Concords Showband £40.

Some months later I booked the noted ballad group to play that same hall in Milltown. They were costing me €50 (£40). It could have been a great night, but unfortunately they called into a pub not far from the venue and after enjoying some beverages they decided to entertain the punters and a great 'seisiun' ensued. But when it came to closing time the majority of punters went home. The well-known ballad group who made their name and fortune singing rebel songs headed down the road to the hall where they performed their usual routine, took their money and went off happy. We had a very small crowd and it was to be many years later before I booked them again. As a group I found them tight when it came to a 'luck penny'. But of course they were only collecting the fee as agreed by their manager and they were not at liberty to tip. Musically, and vocally, they were a great outfit.

Another young group on the cabaret/dance hall circuit back then were The Johnsons. They were a folk/ballad outfit. I booked them for Milltown Hall. The group who were doing a guest appearance at the dance were chatting amongst themselves and tuning up when the door opened and this guy walked in and got a great reception from all of The Johnsons. About 15 minutes before they went on stage, one of The Johnsons approached me and asked if it was okay if their friend Paul, the guy who had just arrived, could go on stage with them. I told them that I couldn't care less if their mother went on with them so long as it didn't cost me any more money than the agreed fee. Paul went on stage with The Johnsons and I doubt very much if one punter even realised he was on stage. To this day the majority of them still don't know that the Paul in question was in fact Paul Brady. He went on to become an artist of international renown, and also a noted song-writer. Tina Turner recorded his song *Paradise Is Here*. I can always boast that Brady performed for me for free! I mentioned it to Paul Brady when I bumped into him at the funeral of the renowned Dublin ballad singer Ronnie Drew. He couldn't even recall it.

Another great money-spinner at dances back then was the mineral bar where we flogged poor-quality soft drinks at exorbitant prices. If the mineral bar wasn't moving fast enough I would always tell the man in the chipper van to increase the amount of salt he was putting on the chips to make the punters more thirsty.

CHAPTER 4

Dancing And Fighting

At The Crossroads

DANCE promoting in the late '60s and early '70s brought mixed fortunes. Because I was then living in County Kildare, I tended to concentrate on Kildare venues. It had one serious drawback. It seemed to me that it was by far the worst county in Ireland for dance hall punch-ups and mid-Kildare was particularly bad. Conversations about a dance in Kildare town, Newbridge or Kilcock the next day would usually start with the question, *"Were there many rows?"*

Dance hall rows in the Kildare/Newbridge areas were put down to the fact that your punters were a mixture of soldiers and jockeys. You had both in big numbers because the towns are situated either side of the Curragh plain, with its sprawling military base and racehorse training stables. It was said that bringing soldiers and jockeys together was as potentially explosive a mix as petrol and a match. But Kilcock and Rathcoffey in north Kildare were also notorious. I often thought that if I was building a cabaret lounge or a dance hall back then that I would add on a fighting room. Although far removed from the area now, I'm told the situation has greatly improved.

Edenderry, just across the border in County Offaly, was no better. I don't think I ever promoted or even attended a dance in Edenderry Town Hall that hadn't had a row. It was essential, when calculating your expenses for promoting a dance in Edenderry Town Hall, to allow for window breakage and glass replacement. The actual dance hall within the Town Hall was situated on the top floor and necessitated bands having to carry their gear up granite steps. It was back-breaking and bands hated playing there. Joe Dolan is one of the many artists who cut their teeth in this venue. Joe played there on Tuesday nights early on in his career for the princely sum of £15. With his charisma, magnetic personality and powerful singing voice, Joe went on to become one of Ireland's best-loved entertainers, and there was much grief when he died, aged only 68, in 2007.

I had some success here with bands and entertainers like Johnny McEvoy, who was the most reliable of them all from a financial point of view. I never lost money on McEvoy, who came from Banagher, County Offaly and who made a huge impact with songs like *Mursheen Durkin* and *Black Velvet Band*. In addition he had one of the most sincere and decent managers in the business, Tom Costello, a Mayo man. I can remember one night we had the late Doc Carroll and *The Royal Blues* from Mayo playing at the Town Hall. I remember it not because of the attendance or the music or the rows, but because they were accompanied by a young guy who pestered me all night to hire his band called *Time Machine*. This guy was about 15 or 16 years old and he was determined that he and his Time Machine were going places. He even engraved his name and phone number on the plastered walls inside the pay box and the details remained there until recent renovations took place. His name was Louis Walsh. Louis, from Kiltimagh, County Mayo, went on to become one of the best-known showbiz managers in Ireland and the UK, steering artists like Boyzone, Westlife and Jedward to international success and appearing as a judge with the likes of pop guru Simon Cowell on The X Factor. It's a long way from the Town Hall in Edenderry to The X Factor!

Marquee dancing was big in our area, but of course the three biggest venues in the country that time were Pilltown in Kilkenny, Ballygar in Galway and Tullamore Harriers. I promoted marquee dancing in Rathangan and Allenwood in County Kildare. On one occasion I brought Dickie Rock to Rathangan. Dickie, a true blue Dub, is one of the legends of Irish popular music and is still filling dance floors to this day. He was the lead singer with the hugely popular *Miami Showband*, and was famous for hits like *Every Step of the Way* and *From the Candy Store on the Corner*. Although some considered he was on the decline at the time, local people just couldn't believe that the renowned Dickie was coming to their little village. But on the day in question clouds also arrived and by 4pm the rain was absolutely pissing down. About an hour before Dickie was due to take the stage, the marquee started to leak and we were fearful that it might interfere with the power supply, or that it might leave the stage's electrical cables too dangerous. Back then people joined electrical wires and often left them totally stripped. It might have been potentially lethal but back in those innocent days before the health and safety culture took hold, you took your chances.

The night was something of a disaster. But the weather improved and Con Hynes from Portumna, from whom we had hired the marquee, sent us a replacement tent the following day. Within a day of the festival finishing I had a bill from Con Hynes. He was looking for his full amount with no discount for Dickie's night, which had really affected the attendance for the remaining dances. When I made this complaint to Mr Hynes he said that I should have called off the festival after the opening night. I replied that I was obliged in law to minimise my loss. He wondered how a young guy like me (then aged about 20) knew the law. I didn't. My solicitor friend, the late Tim O'Toole, drafted the letter for me. I reached an agreement that satisfied me and half-satisfied Hynes.

In October 1972 I had been running a marquee in Allenwood near Naas, County Kildare. It was due to close but when I heard that the Offaly-Kerry All-Ireland football final replay was fixed for the following week, I decided to extend my festival by one week to cater for the Offaly fans on their way home from the match in Croke Park. A great majority of Offaly fans would be making their way home via Allenwood. That was long before the N4 existed and most people from north Offaly went to Dublin via Derrinturn, Allenwood, Prosperous etc. If Offaly won, and they did, the fans might decide to celebrate in Allenwood as they loved to rub it in to old rivals Kildare at the earliest opportunity. This hatred existed from 1961 when Kildare fans hoisted Down flags after the Northern side beat Offaly in the All-Ireland football final.

But greed reared its ugly head! I also booked the Town Hall in Daingean in County Offaly and booked Pat McGarr and the *Gallowglass Ceili Band* to play there. The Gallowglass were probably the most commercially successful ceili band of all time. If I didn't catch the fans in Allenwood I might get them in Daingean with the Gallowglass! In addition to that, our own prodigy at that time, five-year-old Michael Landers and his Big Band, were opening Crookstown Marquee Festival of Dancing in South Kildare. This was going to be some night! But it all went horribly wrong.

The marquee in Allenwood enjoyed a big crowd, but a row broke out and the damage caused to the marquee amounted to more than the profits that were made. The weather turned sour early that Sunday evening and Crookstown Marquee blew away and ended up in the adjoining field. The dance was transferred to the tiny community hall that was hardly big enough to hold the committee and the night was a complete flop. My Ceili in Daingean was a disaster. It appears that Daingean GAA had intended to hold a celebration dance there that night and the people of the town were a bit soured that I got in before the club and booked the hall. What a disastrous night! Offaly fans were celebrating across the county and here was I losing money hand over fist.

One of my biggest promotions each year was staging Joe Dolan in Lawlor's Ballroom in Naas on Easter Saturday. It was a standing order. Each year around February or March the posters would arrive. There was no agreement in writing and it was an understood arrangement that Joe's band *The Drifters* would get 60 per cent of the gross receipts. There was no need for a guarantee as Dolan would pack the place. Their manager Seamus Casey was one of the straightest managers in the business and dealing with him was always a pleasure. Seamus is a gentleman, and unlike other managers of the time he didn't hang around ballrooms as the majority of band managers did, particularly the Dublin based managers. Some of them were back-stabbers, and Seamus Casey wouldn't fit in. The business had its share of sharks and crooks and for a multi-million pound industry back then it was scarce on brains. When I questioned Seamus Casey one time as to why he didn't attend the Dublin gigs he told me that he hated Dublin that much that he went once a year just to remind himself not go again.

Lawlor's Ballroom, a landmark venue, was most respectable but the owners drove a hard bargain. They supplied the staff, including a person to operate the box office, but they extracted an enormous fee. The box office was operated by an elderly lady by the name of Mrs Delaney. What a gentle soul and an extremely honest lady! The only good thing about running a dance here was that you didn't have to be there until the final minutes to collect your money and pay the band. That suited me fine. I was more into money than music at the time and I didn't want to listen to any artist. The money for the ballroom would be taken out first, and you got what was left. Then the band wanted 60 per cent of the gross receipts. It was upsetting to watch thousands of people pay in and then to end up with a few paltry pounds.

I can still vividly recall arriving in Naas on the last night that I promoted Dolan there. It was around 1am and I was travelling alone, having dashed there from Edenderry where I was now entertainments manager of The Copper Beech cabaret lounge, which was also packed out for a show that night. Naas was full of people, and I had great difficulty parking. I was delighted and thought how lucky I was at the age of 23 to be filling the town of Naas and Edenderry on an Easter Saturday through entertainment. But in reality the Naas gig was worth very little financially. That night the band's fee of 60 per cent amounted to £527. That was a lot of money in 1973. I had it rolled up with an elastic band around it and Joe Dolan's brother Ben made a beeline for me as soon as he came off stage. I handed him the bundle and he locked himself into the toilet cubicle in the dressing room to count it. Normally the band would have their own representative in the pay box but Mrs Delaney was such a trusted person that there was no need for anyone to be there. I was wondering about the 'luck money'. I knew that out of the sum of £527 there was no way he would settle for the £500 and give me the £27, but surely to God after all the years trading he would give me the £7! He finally emerged from the toilet cubicle smiling from ear to ear and shoved something into my jacket pocket and said, *"Happy Easter"*. I couldn't wait for him to disappear so I could check out what he had given me. I was so disappointed to find a lousy £2 in my pocket. I had just watched 1,650 people dancing the night away and I end up with little more than £200.

It's amazing how a 'luck penny' can mean so much and when I was still only 18 years old and booking the bands for the marquee festival of dancing in Rathangan I was thrilled when the manager of *The Firehouse Five Showband*, Donie Cassidy, gave me ten shillings out of their fee of £35 for a Sunday night gig. Of course Donie, who later became a Senator and a TD, was ensuring a date at the following year's event. But things ended differently some years later when he invited me and my fiancee to lunch at the Royal Dublin Hotel. I had arranged to meet Brendan Bowyer there to interview him for a *Sunday World* article on Bowyer's 21 years in the business. My appointment with Brendan, who was staying at the Royal Dublin, was for 2pm. Donie Cassidy had made a 1pm lunch appointment. The purpose of Donie's meeting was to promote a record released by the Firehouse Showband entitled *Welcome John Paul*. The song as sung by the band's vocalist Jim Tobin had been released to coincide with the historic visit to Ireland of Pope John Paul II a month earlier. Donie was pushing for an article in the *Sunday World*. This article wasn't on. The Pope was long since gone. To me it was like promoting a Christmas release in January. As 2pm approached, Bowyer's manager at the time, the legendary T.J. Byrne, appeared and reminded me that Brendan had a game of golf arranged and was expecting me at 2pm on the button. I left the table to go to the men's room before joining Bowyer in his suite. I bumped into an old friend on my way to the toilet and got somewhat delayed. On my return I met my fiancee Eileen (now my wife) who asked me where Donie Cassidy had gone. I was puzzled because I had left them all in the restaurant. *"Well Mr Cassidy is gone and there is a girl looking for £16,"* Eileen explained. I didn't have sixteen pence but luckily Eileen had collected her wages before leaving work that day. I had really learned that there was no such thing as a free lunch. With all the talking and the buzz that was about that day Donie had forgotten to pay the bill!

Donie has since enjoyed phenomenal success both in the entertainments industry and in politics. He has successfully won both Senate and Dail seats, has successfully managed that world-famous duo *Foster & Allen*, and has built up a flourishing business in the hotel and record shop sectors. There are many stories told about Donie in both the political and entertainment worlds. Like the one where he was out canvassing in the wilds of County Westmeath on a summer's evening. It was nearing the end of the day when Donie and his canvassers arrived at a country boreen. Donie asked if anyone lived down that boreen and he was told there was an old woman, but it was a long way down and everyone was tired, thirsty and pissed-off. It had been a long day. But Donie realised that one vote could make all the difference. Off they trod down the boreen and found the old lady living alone in rather primitive conditions. It turned out that she had no bathroom, no toilet and no running water. But to Donie this was *"no problem"*. Donie said he was *"appalled"* to learn of her situation and told her that as soon as the elections were over she would have her toilet, her bathroom as well as hot and cold water. He took her name, shook her hand tightly, and was just departing when the old lady asked, *"What party would youse be from now?"*

"Oh, Fianna Fail, Ma'am," replied Donie politely, the eyes blinking in his head like a bulb about to blow.

The old lady took one look at him and shouted, *"Get out*

of the yard yez shower of hoors as quick as yez can. I'd sooner die with the bucket rim marks on me arse than vote for you shower."

CHAPTER 5

Come To The Cabaret

I WAS very interested when I heard that a new cabaret lounge was being built in my home town of Edenderry (population 3,500 in 1972). I was even more interested when I heard it was being built by the O'Brien Group who practically had the town wrapped up from a business point of view, their business activities covering supermarkets, hardware, builder's providers, undertakers, pubs, grains, seeds, fertilisers.

They couldn't go wrong whether you lived or died. But their only involvement in the entertainment world was the Savoy Cinema. I had worked in their Builders' Providers/ Hardware as a young lad and now I was going to approach them with a view to looking after the entertainment in their latest venture. I had the knowledge, and the neck, and so I applied for the job and was successful. I had a meeting with Eugene O'Brien, who had taken over the empire from his father, and Eugene was a very go-ahead guy, but he didn't suffer fools gladly. He was a gentleman, most approachable and a good listener. I assured him I'd do a good, honest job, and today, 40 years later, I believe that I kept all my promises.

But this was no ordinary cabaret lounge. This premises was about 50 years ahead of its time in layout and decor. I used to get a great kick out of watching entertainers arrive at the venue, particularly Dublin-based groups. Some of them believed they were coming down to play in some sort of shack in the bog. But when they stepped in and saw this venue they were clearly gobsmacked. There was no venue like it in Dublin or Cork or any other Irish city or town. I had earlier travelled to England and Scotland with the five-year-old singing star Michael Landers and I had seen nothing like it across the water either. They came from all over Ireland to see The Copper Beech. Wouldn't anyone be proud to be Entertainments Manager of such an establishment? At 23 years of age it was an exciting challenge.

In addition to cabaret acts, the venue had many uses including fashion shows, auctions, bingo and international boxing. Several top-class boxing tournaments were staged there including full internationals with visits from Canadian, American, English and Scottish teams. The top two national boxing reporters back then were Tom Cryan from the *Irish Independent* and Peader O'Brien from *The Irish Press*. In that era the telephone system in Edenderry was a manual system. You turned the crank on the phone and hoped that the local Post Office would answer you, and more importantly, would have sufficient lines available to connect you. It's hard to believe that we're talking mid-1970s and not mid-1870s. There was one phone in The Copper Beech which I kept free for one reporter and I arranged for the use of a second phone at Pat Larkin's Pub across the road for the second reporter. The reporters were very lucky in that I always had an interest in journalism and I knew the ropes (no pun intended) and realised what deadlines meant. They were also lucky in that the person manning the Edenderry Post Office switchboard was either my younger brother Seamus or my brother-in-law, Tom Reilly. Of course the then postmistress, the late Peggy Phelan, or her husband Sean were also most obliging. So we had the communications end of it sorted. The lads got their stories in on time and had enough time left for a few pints before heading back to base.

The boxing ring used in The Copper Beech was the property of the local St Brigid's Boxing Club. It was the same ring that had been used in Croke Park for the famous Muhammed Ali versus Al *'Blue'* Lewis fight in July 1972. The backbone of the Edenderry club was the Brereton brothers, Willie, Sean and Joe, and the younger generation of Breretons who took part in the tournaments then included Irish senior champion Sean and his younger brother Martin, the latter representing Ireland in the Olympic Games in Moscow.

Another young guy who took part back then was a chap from Clones by the name of Barry McGuigan. His dad, Pat, was a very good friend of mine over many years and he led a cabaret group called *Pat McGeegan and the Big Four*. (He performed under the name McGeegan). Some years earlier, in 1968, Pat had represented Ireland in the Eurovision Song Contest with a song entitled *Chance of a Lifetime*. He did very well in the contest, held in London that year, taking fourth place. Now the Copper Beech was the chance of a lifetime for his son!

After the gig at The Copper Beech, Pat McGuigan would stay on chatting and he became very friendly with our security man Joe Brereton. No-one would get a word in after the gig when Joe and Pat got together, with the exception of course of our general manager Pat Tyrrell.

Pat had been an amateur boxer and boxing was his first love. During one of the many conversations Pat McGuigan had asked if young Barry could be included in one of the forthcoming boxing tournaments. Pat was so impressed with the vibrancy and strength of the Edenderry Boxing Club that he even considered selling out his business in Clones and coming to live in Edenderry. He knew his son had potential and he wanted only the best for him. The Edenderry Club was, as a far as Pat McGuigan was concerned, the best in the land at the time. When Barry was still only a 14 years old I was told by one of the Brereton brothers that this young kid was no ordinary boxer. Tommy 'Snowball' Brereton, who lived in London, flew over to see his nephew Sean box at Dublin's National Stadium in an International against Germany. The following day I asked Tommy if he had seen a young guy called McGuigan from County Monaghan fight the night before. I would always have valued Snowball's opinion on boxers. He looked me and without hesitation replied, *"Yes, I saw him. He's a young Marciano!"* Barry fought as a juvenile in the Copper Beech in 1974 — he would have been about 13 at the time.

Later in the decade, Barry won the All-Ireland Amateur Championship, having defeated Martin Brereton. Known as the Clones Cyclone, Barry went on to become one of the world's top professional boxers, winning 32 of his 35 fights, and becoming world featherweight champion.

The late Pat McGuigan and I became close friends and I spent many happy days and nights in Clones with him and his family. The McGuigan family were the salt of the earth, and I really enjoyed how they argued over who would serve a customer in their busy little shop in The Diamond. A bell would ring when a customer entered, and then the argument would start in their adjoining kitchen, *"No, I'm not going. Let Barry go, I went the last time.*" I was really saddened by the death of Pat. He was a lovely man, a great father and husband. I still make contact with his drummer Gerry Douglas, who also lives in Clones.

The General Manager of The Copper Beech, Pat Tyrrell, was a God-fearing man. He was so honest and honourable that some of the things he did were unbelievable, if not, at times, laughable. We became very close friends and I still miss him. I can recall on one occasion he was so embarrassed at ordering toilet roll holders for the men's toilet that he took the one from his own bathroom and used it in The Copper Beech. There was this particular guy who just broke them off to torment Pat, and we believe he did it for no other reason. Of course we had another two scumbags who came to a cabaret one night armed with screwdrivers and when the opportunity presented itself they removed an interior toilet door off its hinges. We found out many years later who they were. Pat Tyrrell would spend hours on end repairing such wanton destruction of one of the most modern lounges in Europe. I can still see him sitting on the edge of the stage one afternoon spending hours unravelling Christmas Fairy Lights from the previous year when all he had to do was lift the phone and order new ones. If the thirst got the better of him and he took a small Britvic Orange he would open his wallet and pay one of the staff or record it himself and put the money in the cash register. He never touched alcohol.

Pat approached me one morning and he was out of breath. I thought something serious had just occurred. After composing himself some he told me that a man had called looking for a booking. It turned out that the artist was the hypnotist Paul Golden. *"He sat there at the end of the counter and he broke silver tea spoons as if they were match sticks,"* said

Pat, and he was still shaking from the ordeal. I was thrilled and was looking forward to contacting him for a date or series of dates. Then Pat continued, *"Don't bring that 'hoor' around here. That fella is not right. There's a divil in that lad as big as a dog. The place could fall if we let him perform here."*

It took me days to persuade Pat to allow me book Paul Golden. I couldn't care less if there were ten "divils" in him. I knew he would be a big attraction and at the end of the day it was my job to fill the place. Paul Golden did just that for three nights in a row and had dozens of punters running around the town looking for leprechauns. In one instance a guy was found in an adjoining pub after closing hours by an over-officious garda who later summonsed him. There was great laughter (and national publicity) when the case came before the local District Court. There was an outburst of laughter when the late and legendary solicitor Tim O'Toole asked the defendant to tell the court what he was doing in Larkin's pub after hours. *"Looking for a leprechaun,"* replied the defendant. The late District Justice Bill Tormey, who enjoyed the colourful antics of solicitor O'Toole was anxious to keep it going. The laughter continued unabated when O'Toole extracted from the defendant that he was, in fact, a teetotaller. When Judge Tormey, who was a great character and a man of great compassion, eventually composed himself he said, *"We'll blame this Mr Golden fella"* as he applied the Probation Act.

Despite it being the early to mid-1970s, The Copper Beech, located in a town on the road to nowhere in particular, operated seven nights a week. Thankfully we had a good catchment area, for if we had been depending on Edenderry people it would not have been the success that it was. We did a sort of an amateur survey one time and it showed that more than 60 per cent of the patrons were from outside the town.

Apart from the boxing tournaments, my interest in journalism came to good use on another occasion while operating at the Copper Beech. It was the evening in December 1972 when two bombs believed to have been planted by Northern Ireland loyalists went off in Dublin and RTE journalists were on strike.

Worse was to follow a couple of years later with the Dublin/Monaghan bombings that claimed the lives of dozens of victims. But back in 1972 the idea of bombs going off in Ireland's capital city still came as a huge shock to people.

Rumours and counter-rumours abounded throughout The Copper Beech that night about the number of dead and injured, and the rumours were all stemming from people from the town who were working in the city. It eing a Friday, they were arriving home for the weekend and they all had different versions of what had happened. I got the idea of phoning the *Irish Independent* just before 11pm and, explaining who I was, asked to be put through to the News Editor. The newsdesk man on duty was most courteous, most understanding and gave me a reasonably good run-down on the situation. I scribbled it down, had a brief look at it before I went on stage to wrap up proceedings for the night. As I got silence for the National Anthem I proceeded to announce the latest account of the Dublin bombings. It emerged that two Dublin bus conductors had been killed. You could have heard a pin drop. I received a prolonged round of applause. It was a strange feeling, particularly after some of the details I had just announced. For weeks after people stopped me in the street to compliment me.

When things went quiet mid-week in The Copper

Beech, one had to dream up some scheme to attract punters and over the years we were running thin on ideas. Talent contests were good for attracting a crowd but had been overdone, and getting adjudicators was always a problem. A contest usually ended in a dispute and decent people who would oblige you by acting as adjudicators ended up being attacked and verbally abused. On one occasion we had to stop an adjudicator from being assaulted.

It was around the mid-1970s and I decided we would run a talent contest on a small scale. We would have a "once-off" each Thursday night. No second round, no quarter-finals, just a winner and runner-up on the night. To help boost the attendance, I decided on an audience vote. So if you were going to perform and you wanted to be in with a shout you brought along all your pals, family etc. Although it was really amateurish I still insisted on getting some details from the contestants, even ones I knew personally, so that I could introduce them with some sort of spiel and make it look and sound a bit professional.

I was standing at the side of the stage one night listening to some contestant strangling a song when this young guy approached me with a Dublin accent. For some reason or other I was in a foul mood. *"Excuse me sir, can me friend sing?"* he roared into my ear. *"I don't know,"* I shouted back, *"I never heard him."*

"Oh, Jaysus Mister he's bleedin brilliant. Honestly Mister." I told him to tell his friend to go into the dressing room and wait there. Eventually I arrived into the dressing room and this tall guy with long blond hair was looking down at me. He put out his hand and said, *"Thank you very much. I'm so thankful that you allowed me enter the competition."*

I knew from that very second I was dealing with both a gentleman, and someone special. As I was taking down some details, he interrupted to say, *"My dad sang here."* He explained that his dad was the renowned tenor Patrick O'Hagan (real name, Charles Sherrard). This was a man who had performed three times at the White House, for John F. Kennedy, Lyndon B. Johnson and Richard Nixon. *"Jaysus"*, I said, as I started to take a note. *"That's great."*

"Excuse me Mister," he said, *"I'd prefer if you didn't mention my dad. That wouldn't be fair to the other contestants. My name is Sean O'Hagan, just leave it at that."* He had confirmed my first impressions. As my late mother used say, *"An ounce of breeding is worth a ton of feeding."*

The contest proceeded and Sean O'Hagan's performance almost lifted the roof. But unfortunately for him he hadn't brought enough people with him, and a local and popular barman Peadar O'Neill picked up the first prize of five punts (€6.30) with Sean O'Hagan, or Johnny Logan, as he would later be known, taking second place and receiving four punts (€5.06). For years we slagged Peadar O'Neill, while he still brags about beating Johnny Logan in a talent competition. Ironically, when Logan came to play in The Copper Beech after winning the Eurovision Song Contest at The Hague in 1980 with *What's Another Year*, it was four punts admission fee. He went on to win the Eurovision a second time, in 1987, with *Hold Me Now*.

On the night of that talent contest, Sean O'Hagan stayed on after closing time and he told me that he was an apprentice electrician and was working in town at the wiring of an IDA advance factory. He said that he had run short of money and when his friend saw the poster for the talent contest he persuaded Sean to take part. We drank the prize money that night and the singer who became Johnny Logan was to become one of the biggest attractions at the venue, and we have been good friends ever since.

Two artists I always enjoyed seeing at the Copper were comedian Brendan Grace and ballad singer Paddy Reilly. Back then, they arrived with nothing more than a guitar under their arm and they gave a great performance. Afterwards they would join in the craic with the staff and both of them at times would take out their guitars and entertain us until well into the next day. Brendan Shine was also good fun and on one occasion when Pat Tyrrell's wife Maura arrived after hours with a pot of rabbit soup, Shine scoffed most of it. Locally there was a great artist from Clara called 'Ricey' Scully who was well-known across the Midlands and still has his own show on Midlands Radio 3. He was a member of *The Crackerjacks* showband in the 1960s. He could dream up novel ideas for concerts and cabarets in seconds. He now fronted a group called *The Twiggs*. They were on stage during a charity gig at the Copper one night and were into their third number before I realised that Ricey was missing. Then the band stopped and requested that the exit door be opened as someone was trying to get in. Some punter opened the door and in comes Ricey Scully riding a donkey and wearing a sombrero with a shawl or "poncho" over his shoulders. The audience was in uproar and the poor auld ass reacted accordingly. He crossed the carpet section without difficulty but it was when he landed on the maple dance floor he had difficulty finding his footing. He was skidding in all directions and, overcome with sheer fright, he did his number one and his number two in the middle of the maple floor. Manager Pat Tyrrell didn't know whether to laugh or cry, but the only thing that really annoyed him was the fact that the owner of the ass had been barred from the premises.

****

The people of Edenderry are well-known for their charity and Monday nights were always set aside for charity gigs. Local artists performed at the drop of a hat to help out many causes. Such was their willingness that all I had to do was print up the poster and when they'd see their name in print they'd all turn up. I doubt if many towns could make that boast. Those same artists, some now gone to the next world, never sought anything in return. They helped pay many funeral expenses. They put food on tables that would otherwise have been bare. They made Christmas a reality for many a child and many a family, and they raised thousands for the local Lourdes fund as well as for missionaries around the world. In 2001 we formed a small committee in Edenderry to remember our past entertainers and on May 31, 2010 we became the first town in Ireland to erect a monument to the deceased entertainers. It stands proudly in the local St Mary's Parish cemetery. For me it was an ambition fulfilled.

****

It was after closing time at The Copper Beech one night and the staff were enjoying a well-earned drink while manager Pat Tyrrell was checking the premises and clearing the cash registers. I got a strong smell of rubber burning but it took me some time to discover that it was coming from a cooler underneath the counter. I knew nothing about coolers, other than what it said on the tin; they cooled the beer. There was clearly some kind of electrical fault. The situation got worse and I phoned the post office next door and spoke with Sean Phelan, who was the husband of postmistress Peggy Phelan. He told me that his lights had also been dimming. They had a manual phone system and the local exchange had to connect you to any number you wanted to call in the town and surrounding areas. I asked him to put me through to the takeaway the other side of the Copper and I spoke with proprietor Val Tyrrell. He told me that his lights had been flickering for a period and now he was in the dark. Without hesitation I asked the exchange to put me through to the Garda station. I knew something strange was happening.

I eventually spoke with Sergeant John Reilly who was in fact in bed, having been out socialising earlier that night. He told me to stay put that he was on his way. It emerged that a criminal gang had been trying to disrupt the power supply in the town, presumably to facilitate a break-in without the alarm going off.

John Reilly was one of the old stock, perhaps the last of the real community gardai. Sergeant Reilly, a Longford native, had served in Donegal and Daingean, County Offaly before coming to Edenderry. He was a tough but fair man, not afraid of anyone or anything. He had no tolerance for criminals, didn't mind the man who had a drink after hours, and wasn't too pushed about the guy who couldn't afford to tax his car, but would take very seriously anyone driving without insurance. Like all men in such positions he had his enemies, as is understandable, but I always found him to be extremely fair, and a good friend. The men who served with him were also fine individuals. They were all stationed in the town for years. We grew up with them. They socialised with the local people. They played sports with the locals, were part of the GAA and boxing clubs. They played football, they trained teams. When a crime was committed it didn't take them long to solve it. They had a community fully behind them.

Within five minutes of calling Sergeant Reilly that night, I observed the garda car pass by our premises on Main Street and proceed towards O'Connell Square located another hundred yards further on. As the squad car entered the square a vehicle took off at high speed driving back down the Main Street and taking a sharp right turn towards Kinnegad. Sergeant Reilly gave chase, but pulled in at The Copper Beech to pick me up, and we were also joined by our security man Joe Brereton and Val Tyrrell from the local takeaway. We sped out the Kinnegad road and I noticed as I put on the seat belt in the front passenger seat that there was a shotgun there. I had consumed four or five pints and was in great form for action. About a mile out the road, we noticed a car coming towards us. I suggested to Sgt Reilly that we should pull in and stop the approaching car and ask the driver if he had seen the vehicle that we were chasing. John brought the patrol car to a halt and stepped out in an attempt to stop the oncoming car. What a narrow escape! As it approached us, it increased speed and we then discovered it was the gang we were after, who had doubled back. I jumped out of the garda car and tried to take out the shotgun, but it got caught in the door and the gang was a mile away within minutes. As we turned and chased them back towards town I was on the car radio calling for assistance from any station that might be listening. I'm sure the gardai were amused, as I didn't have the lingo they use and I was half-pissed as well. They couldn't be blamed for thinking that the patrol car had been stolen. The gang was eventually caught near Maynooth in County Kildare as they tried to make their way back to Dublin. They were taken to Naas Garda Station.

We often thought and talked about the incident over the years. What would have happened had I managed to get the shotgun out of the garda car and discharged a shot? It doesn't bear thinking about. We learned that the gang were targeting McGreal's Jewellers Shop on Edenderry's Main

Street and had been throwing something over the high tension wires in O'Connell Square trying to black-out the entire town. That is what caused the flickering of the lights at the Post Office and the black-out in the takeaway, and made the coolers in the Copper act up as they did. I never did find out the origin of the shotgun or how it got into the garda car. But I do recall Sergeant Reilly saying to me on a number of occasions, *"If I ever get a call to set-up a road block, they needn't think I'm going to do it armed with just a pot stick."*

My first real meeting with Sergeant Reilly occurred one day when I was in serious trouble over a bar licence for The Copper Beech. We had an international boxing tournament coming up and we required a bar extension. I had totally overlooked the matter until manager Pat Tyrrell asked me on the evening of court day if the licence had been granted. I told him it had and he was delighted. It hadn't even been applied for. I had totally forgotten about it. Now I was in deep trouble. I didn't know which direction to turn. Number one, we had no extension, and worse still I had told a blatant lie. But had I told Pat the truth he would have freaked. He panicked for very little. He was so anxious that if a top group cancelled, I'd book a replacement before telling him of the cancellation. I gave the licence (or no licence) problem some thought but decided that I couldn't delay too long.

I slept on it that night and the next morning I decided to confront it head-on. I went directly to the Garda station to have a quiet word with Sergeant Reilly. I had been told he was a fair man. Now I was going to put his fairness to the test. Luck was on my side for when I arrived at the station he was all alone. He gave me a friendly greeting and told me to take a seat. I told him the situation. He stood up from his desk and went to a cupboard from where he took down a big book, opened it, looked at me and asked, *"Who knows about this?"*

"Just me, and now you," I said. He scribbled something into the book before putting it back into the press and said, *"That licence was granted yesterday. I'll see you on the night. It should be a great night's boxing."*

John Reilly loved his pint of Guinness and I made sure he got his quota on the night of the tournament. I went a step further. I invited him to address the huge audience as our *"chief of police"* and to formally welcome the Canadian team and entourage to Edenderry. He was thrilled, but not half as much as I was.

CHAPTER 6

The Boy Wonder

HAVING used showband *The Concords* for a few gigs I became friendly with the members and with their manager Sean Judge. Soon I was helping out with getting gigs for them, doing press releases and generally hanging out with all of them. In 1968 the Kildare-based band was booked for a series of dates in Aviemore in Scotland. They played in a tiny hall in Bracknagh in north Offaly the previous night. Our kitchen was bigger than this venue but The Concords were thrilled when they filled it. After the gig we set off for Larne to get the ferry to Stranraer but when we arrived in Larne we were told that because of a foot-and-mouth outbreak we could not take our vehicle on board. We had no alternative but carry on the gear and hope that we would secure transport on the far side. We had plenty of help, for at this stage the band was top heavy with members, managers and followers.

We secured transport and drove in blizzard conditions to Aviemore where the band performed in the Osprey Rooms. I have very little recollection of that trip or the gig other than the cable cars where we spent a few enjoyable hours. A coach took us back to the port at Stranraer and I do recall the driver standing up and asking, *"Who pays me?"* That was the joke of the trip. I still don't know why I said it, but I remember replying, *"That's one for Ireland's Own."* He took our details and pursued us for the money. He was paid in full.

The Concords engaged many fine singers but none of them was capable of making the breakthrough, or perhaps more accurately, the management (including myself) didn't have the money or the know-how to make it into the big time or get that lucky break. Only recently I was astounded when my good friend Eddie Rowley of the *Sunday World* hit me with a statistic. *"Only one in 10,000 make it,"* he said.

We were financially incapable of matching the bigger outfits that had the dosh to pay for radio plays and newspaper publicity. Payola was rife in Ireland back then. However, a breakthrough did materialise and we certainly made the news, not just in Ireland but across Europe. The person who made all that difference was our new lead vocalist named Michael Landers. The lad from Kilcullen in County Kildare was all of five years old.

My business partner Sean Judge had heard about young Michael from a neighbour, Liz Slattery, who had heard the kid performing at a wedding in O'Neill's pub in Milltown, County Kildare. This young boy had been called on to perform at this wedding bash and had brought the place down. Sean checked him out and within hours had landed on his doorstep in Kilcullen. His mother was very anxious that her son's talents be fully recognised and realised.

She was a lovely person who never stopped smiling and was so proud of all her children. Some of them were members of the local Narraghmore Pipe Band as well as being very talented Irish dancers. Young Michael had the mum's winning smile and a twinkle in his eye that would win the heart of anyone. He was extremely well-mannered and an extremely intelligent kid. It didn't take us long to get him organised and standing on stage doing rehearsals with The Concords showband in an old hall on the banks of the Grand Canal in Allenwood, northwest Kildare. But there were lots of things that we didn't allow for. We never allowed for the fact that at five years of age Michael couldn't read so we had to teach him the song words line-by-line. This is where his sister Jennifer came in, and she also travelled to the gigs with him. Before we met him he had learned a ditty recorded back then by a band called *The Hoedowners,* entitled *The Poor Poor Farmer*. The John F. Kennedy Hall in Michael's native Kilcullen was located on the same narrow laneway as the Lander's home and he had rambled up on an occasion when The Hoedowners were playing in the hall and somehow secured a copy of the disc.

Michael's dad Tom Landers was a sergeant in the Military Police stationed at the nearby Curragh Camp. We often wondered if he was happy with Michael making his career as an entertainer. While I am sure Tom did his job with efficiency and courtesy, a few of his colleagues in the Military Police were as popular around the Curragh that time as the B-Specials were on the Falls Road in Belfast. I was unfortunate enough to be stopped by them on numerous occasions. We employed many members of the army band back then. They were all brilliant musicians. Trumpet players like Mick Healy or Toddy Gannon on trombone. It was often my job to drop off the lads at their base at all hours of the night. We were stopped almost every night. Despite the fact that we had the same vehicle, same colour, same registration plate and usually the same driver they insisted on asking the same questions. I found them the most arrogant security force I ever encountered, and that includes the British Army. I do appreciate, however, that they were difficult times in Ireland.

We did realise that somewhere along the line we might be breaking the law by having Michael Landers appear publicly, so Sean Judge contacted the Department of Justice. At the age of 20 we had little knowledge of the law other than we were brought up to abide by it. It was a time when we would cross the street when meeting a garda. Of course that was wrong too! In their ignorance, or lack of interest, or both, the Department of Justice gave us the all-clear and said they could find nothing to prevent young Michael from appearing publicly as an artist. Inexperience prevented us from getting that in writing from the Department, although I doubt if in the end it would have made much difference. When the matter was discussed at rehearsals or while socialising, I would always say that when the Billy Barry Dancers could appear on The Late Late Show we should be OK. We tried but failed to get a spot on the Late Late. In the end young Michael Landers was shafted in an unbelievable and extremely cruel manner.

Apart from the Late Late heads ignoring us, getting publicity for Michael Landers was easy. Every newspaper in the nation wanted to write an article on him. He was something new. Unbelievable really! A five-year-old singer going to front an eight-piece band! A five-year-old singer who had made his first record before making his First Communion! The newspaper articles brought radio interviews and now people were beginning to take notice.

It was time for Michael to make a record. We had been friends of the Kelly brothers, Des and Johnny, who were members of the very successful but now defunct *Capitol*

Showband that had been fronted by the late and legendary Butch Moore. The Kelly brothers were now in the management end of showbiz and owned the new Ruby Record label. They also had in their stable the very talented guitarist and record producer Jerry Hughes. We came across a song entitled *If I Could Be A Sailorman* that had been recorded by another child prodigy called Heintje, who was a Dutch boy. He was not allowed to perform in the Netherlands and had to go to Germany to do so.

We had to teach Michael the words of the song but he was a smart kid and very soon we were ready for the studios. Gerry Hughes looked after the studios and the main session man on the recording was none other than the late accomplished artist and accordion player Dermot O'Brien. The County Louth star believed he had made a mistake by performing on the recording when newspaper articles stated that playing *"second fiddle"* to the young boy was Dermot O'Brien. He refused further studio assignments with Landers. Despite all the publicity, finding solid and suitable gigs proved difficult enough. Promoters and ballroom proprietors couldn't get their heads around a band with a five-year-old singer, and while other bands greeted his arrival with amusement, jealousy wasn't long creeping in and very soon some of them looked on him as a threat.

It was a cut-throat and back-stabbing, dog-eat-dog business with very little brains. The name of the game was bluff, and it was riddled with sharks and chancers waiting to get any individual with talent to sign themselves away. The country had an average of 40 bands for every county. It was like the recent building boom. It created a false economy. It was unreal and of course unsustainable.

Sean Judge called on his Auntie *'Pidge'* Ennis from Rathangan, who was an accomplished dressmaker. He asked her to design something appropriate for the boy. With his debut song being *If I Could Be A Sailorman*, Sean's very talented auntie designed and manufactured a little white sailor suit complete with brass buttons. We started off with gigs in Wexford followed by Kerry and Kildare and Michael was going down a storm. The record made the charts, although radio plays were hard to come by and payola was rife. We were pipped at the post for the number one slot by Brendan Shine who was riding the crest of a wave back then with a ditty called *O'Brien Has No Place To Go*.

We had also secured one of the 15-minute sponsored programmes on RTE Radio. They were extremely popular and we bought the 11.15pm to 11.30pm show on Monday nights. The show was hosted by the man who held the lease at the time, the late Harry Thuillier, a former sports commentator with RTE. Thuillier was actually sub-letting the show to us, which we later discovered was not to RTE's liking. That was no concern of ours and we were paying him €88 (£70) per week, which was a lot of money back in 1971. We also started a fan club and the amount of mail that came in was unreal. Young Michael received cards and letters, including Mass bouquets and Miraculous Medals. We also received a huge amount of letters of protest. Some people felt that it was an absolute disgrace having a young lad of five years of age up in RTE in Donnybrook at half past eleven at night singing his little heart out, when he should be at home in Kilcullen and tucked away in his bed. Of course what they didn't know was that the programme was pre-recorded in the then Eamon Andrews studios at 3pm on a Saturday. But we couldn't answer the critics who objected to him being in a smoke-filled ballroom at 12 o'clock at night in Cork or Donegal. But as far as we were concerned back then, the Department of Justice had given us the green light and his parents (well his mum at least) were happy with our arrangements. His sister Jennifer always travelled with him and Michael was taken to and from the venue mostly by car and seldom in the bandwagon, although he preferred the latter, and the lads all loved him.

This kid was really talented and it was obvious that he was happiest when he was on stage with an eight-piece band belting out the tunes behind him. What would be a disaster for an adult performer turned into a major boost for Michael's appearance one night in Dublin's National Ballroom. I remember that some of the guys in the band had warned him about consuming too much Coca-Cola in the dressing room before he was due to go on stage. Michael was into his fourth number and the massive crowd were lapping him up when, without warning, he stopped singing, started to whinge, and blurted, *"I want to do me wee, wee."* At first the crowd thought it might be part of the act, but it became hilarious when they discovered that he was serious. The performance was halted and Michael went to the loo before returning to rapturous applause.

All the bands added together were not getting the publicity we were now receiving and, better still, we were getting it all for free. But one thing that one didn't get for free back then was radio plays. You made your way to Madigan's Pub in Moore Street in Dublin and it was there you could meet them all. Gangsters of the highest degree. One individual always claimed to have the radio play trade wrapped up. He was so organised that he could give you a hand-written list of the RTE radio programmes that a particular record would be played on after you handed him a considerable amount of money. We never received one of the plays he promised us. He was a miserable, slimy little chancer. I was told later that this guy was asked by bigger fish affected by the arrival of young

Landers not to organise the radio plays.

In 1971, the ballroom business was on the decline and the Landers band was numerically too big to adapt to the cabaret scene, which at that time was only in its infancy. Good gigs were hard to come by but we soldiered on and did the best we could. Our fortunes were mixed. At one stage the BBC sent over a film crew to do a documentary for their current affairs programme, *24 Hours*, on the Boy Wonder from Ireland. The programme was fronted by Bernard Falk, a seasoned reporter who had earlier worked for the *Daily Mirror*. The programme's anchor man was Cliff Michelmore and it was viewed by millions across the UK. It created quite a stir, which in one way worked to our advantage, but they went extremely hard on us and highlighted management as being ruthless and exploiting a five-year-old boy. We toured the UK a short time later and the crowds flocked to the various venues. We also had British police snooping around and we put this down to the exposure on BBC. Ironically, however, the British law that was to prevent Landers from appearing in Ireland had long been repealed in Britain.

We had a capacity crowd at The Carousel Ballroom in Manchester on St Patrick's night, and there was near bedlam when it ended as thousands converged on Michael's dressing room wanting to meet their hero in the flesh and get his autograph. What they didn't realise was that it would take Michael three minutes to sign his name. It resulted in us having to sneak him out through a rear door and get him to his hotel by taxi. I remember that it took us a long time to persuade the punters that Michael Landers had left the building. But unlike Elvis' manager Tom Parker, we were telling the truth. He had left the building. One memory I have of that night is seeing both the late Joe Dolan and Bridie Gallagher pissed in the ballroom bar. As a teetotaller at the time, I wasn't impressed.

What should have been another huge break also fell apart. The *Sunday Mirror* came to visit us and their Dublin reporter, the late Jim Dunne, did a huge spread. It was to be a centre-page colour pull-out printed at their new state-of-the-art printing works in Belfast. It was the only one in Ireland that could do colour back then. Money couldn't buy this publicity. This would have been the envy of every band in Ireland and England. This was massive. We thought Sunday would never come. But the Provisional IRA had different plans. At 4pm on the Saturday the Provos blew the plant away. End of story.

But it was a gig in Westport, County Mayo, that turned out to be the beginning of the end for Michael Landers. I took a phone call from the late Johnny Kelly of Ruby Records telling me that a venue in Westport called the Belclare House Hotel, then owned by the late John Healy, was looking for a band. Kelly warned me of two things. He pointed out that as a venue it was not going well, and that Healy was, to put it mildly, not a man of his word.

"Make sure you get paid," said Johnny. From that moment I had told myself that Mr Healy was not going to "do" me. After phoning Mr Healy we decided on doing the gig and the deal was 50 per cent of the gross receipts with a guarantee of €127 (£100). As Kelly had predicted, the dance was a disaster. Healy disappeared and left 50 per cent of the receipts, mere buttons, with a member of staff. I refused to take the money and demanded to see Mr Healy. I was told he had gone home and was probably in bed. I made it clear that I was not leaving his premises until I got my guaranteed amount.

Eventually, a back door bursts open and John Healy came in like a raging bull. He was dressed in only a shirt and trousers, and I can vividly see him pulling-up his braces, either genuinely or trying to pretend that he had been in bed. He attacked us on approach and wanted to know who wouldn't leave his premises. Trying to reason with him proved fruitless. He lost it and said he had called the Gardai. We thought he was bluffing but he wasn't. Being the big man around town he would have more clout than a showband from the Midlands. Showband people didn't have a great standing in society back then either. Within minutes of his threat to call the Gardai, a young member of the force arrived and he too started shouting as he entered the ballroom. He asked Healy to point out the people who were refusing to leave. I can still clearly see him standing in the ballroom. To me it looked as if he had his hand on his baton and he threatened that he would take swift action if we didn't leave immediately. We decided to leave, but we were so disappointed that the cop didn't even ask us what the problem was. As we left the premises and drove away, the garda and Mr Healy stood grinning.

The following day I wrote letters of complaint about the behaviour of the garda to the sergeant and superintendent in Westport and the chief superintendent in Castlebar. Acknowledgements were received and the then superintendent in Kildare, the late Tom Broderick, was sent out to interview me. He took a statement and told me I was perfectly correct in making the complaint in that the garda in question appeared to be off-side, but before departing he also told me, *"I'm sorry to tell you, and I'm telling you confidentially, this complaint will probably go nowhere."* He was right, and he was wrong! It went somewhere alright. It went all the way to the top, but it went against us.

Within weeks of our complaint we noticed that something was not right. Promoters were using various excuses for not hiring us and it wasn't until a few honest promoters told us that their local gardai had warned them about hiring young Landers and his band. Promoters were told they would be breaking the law and the consequences would be serious. No promoter wanted that shit. But under the particular section, Part C of Section 2 of The Prevention of Cruelty to Children Act, there were no provisions (that we could see) for taking action against the promoter. But having to explain all that to a ballroom proprietor or promoter was not on.

In what was a brave move at the time we arranged to meet a friendly garda who was partial to the odd pint of porter. Truthfully, this guy would drink porter from a whore's boot. The meeting took place in a remote pub and the garda obliged us by taking along a file that had arrived in his station on the Landers saga. We uncovered one single letter that told it all. It was from Garda HQ to a chief superintendent and it read, *"I note from the files of Kevin Farrell that the band in question have a five-year-old singer. Don't you think we have a case here?"*

Believe me they did, and they left no stone unturned in executing it. But in their ignorance or perhaps determination to put us off the road they overlooked a simple law that would prevent any person of the age of Michael Landers to be in a licensed ballroom at night. They mightn't have bothered digging up an act that dated back to 1904. But someone had crawled into the attic and uncovered an act that was brought in by the British government at the turn of the century to protect children who were being sent to circuses and road shows and some being sent down the coal mines in England. The one they produced was Part C of Section 2 of The Prevention of Cruelty to Children Act of 1904.

Ironically, the first prosecution came for an appearance in Carlow and the promoters of the gig were the Carlow branch of the Irish Society for the Prevention of Cruelty to Children. Here we were being prosecuted for raising funds for this particular charity. We were to be convicted as well.

Legendary Laois/Offaly TD Oliver J. Flanagan summed it up best one day in the Dail when he said that gardai from all over the country were converging on every venue where the boy appeared as if he was the US gangster Michael Dillinger and not the innocent five-year-old singer Michael Landers. He was right. Serious crime was on the up-and-up and the gun had now appeared on the streets of Ireland, but the gardai still had time to chase a five-year-old singer around the 26 counties at all hours of the day and night.

This is what the late Deputy Flanagan had to say: *"I would like to ask the Minister for Justice whether, as a result of a recent court decision involving a five-year-old singer (name supplied), it is now proposed to prosecute in the case of all children under the age prescribed by law who appear on stage or other public places to participate in pantomimes and concerts in Dublin theatres and other similar places of entertainment; and if he will make a statement on the matter.*

"There appears to be a very high degree of injustice in regard to this boy, Michael Landers. This five-year-old boy is a very talented singer, extremely well-known throughout the country and also extremely well-known on radio and on records and he is very much sought after."

Minister Robert Molloy: *"What is his name?"*

Mr O.J. Flanagan: *"Michael Landers, the five-year-old wonder boy from Kilcullen, County Kildare. I understand that the Minister will have further information if he looks up Parliamentary Question No. 49 on [1036] Thursday, 5th August, 1971, at column 3524 of the Official Report, where I raised a question in connection with an engagement in Westport, County Mayo. This boy, and the showband with which he was associated, appeared for an engagement in a hotel. Some difficulty arose in regard to the payment of fees. The hotel owner* *hesitated in meeting his obligations with the result that the guards were called. An incident followed. At that time I asked the Minister for Justice to hold an inquiry and I understand some type of inquiry was held but that the evidence of eight witnesses, who were available and brought forward by the manager of Michael Landers, was not seriously considered. The result of the showband manager pressing the case in connection with the Westport incident was that it provoked widespread activity by the entire Garda force. I object seriously, now that we have such a wave of crime, a number of unsolved murders and great public uneasiness regarding the implementation of law and order, that the time of the Garda Siochana, from the commissioner down, should be occupied in following a five-year-old boy around the country.*

"When this boy became associated with a showband his manager got in touch with the Department of Justice and informed them that the showband in question had the named artist appearing on an average of three nights a week. The Department of Justice informed the showband that they could find no law to prevent this boy from appearing. The showband were extremely worried at the time lest they might be breaking the law."

An Ceann Comhairle: *"I am sorry to interrupt the Deputy but the question is if it is now proposed to prosecute in the case of all children. We are not discussing the specific case mentioned by the Deputy which has been determined by the court. The question is: does the Minister propose to prosecute all other children of the same age?"*

Mr O.J. Flanagan: *"That is exactly the point and I agree completely with the Chair. Is there to be a law for Michael Landers alone or is the law to be impartially administered to all others in a similar age group? This is a very serious matter because the Garda authorities have gone out of their way to pick on this boy. I feel I am within the Rules of Order in asking the Minister for Justice why has this boy been singled out, apart from other young people who* participate in concerts, stage shows or in street shows or in Christmas pantomimes? This boy was picked out. I want to accuse the Minister of saying that the law is not being administered impartially in this case, first, because of the Westport incident and, secondly, because the Garda superintendent in my own area, in reference to an appearance on Sunday, 7th May, 1972, in Abbeyleix, caused the local Macra na Feirme to be informed on that day that unless this boy artiste was taken from the list of artistes in the musical event that was to take place in the hall, the hall committee of Macra na Feirme would be prosecuted under the Prevention of Cruelty to Children Act, 1904.

"I should like to hear from the Minister for Justice what authority the Garda authorities had to warn Macra na Feirme in Abbeyleix that if this boy appeared the Macra na Feirme organisation would be prosecuted. This was a form of intimidation. There is no provision under which Macra na Feirme could have been prosecuted in the Cruelty to Children Act, 1904. The Minister must know that. Every member of this House knows it. It was intimidation to prevent this boy from appearing thus causing considerable embarrassment to his parents and family, damaging him in his career as a singer and record-maker, and damaging the reputation of the recording firm that was producing his records for radio purposes. It has been a great worry to his manager, to his parents, friends and admirers. Why is he singled out as Public Enemy No 1 in the country and why should there be a file in every superintendent's office in this State asking the Garda authorities to look out for a showband with which this five-year-old artiste appears? The same precautions seem to have been taken as would have been taken in the United States against Dillinger during his wild days.

"I accuse the Department of Justice of treating this boy in a disgraceful manner. It should be the subject of a serious inquiry. I am not satisfied, more particularly as this showband and this young artiste had just returned from an English tour and, bad *and all as the English laws are, the 1904 Act was not rigidly implemented in Britain in so far as his appearances were concerned.*

It would not have been implemented by any of the Garda superintendents if it were not for the fact that a garda was reported and an inquiry held in Westport, County Mayo. This has been responsible for it. If we are to have respect for the Garda force there must not be victimisation. This has been a clear case of victimisation.

"Now that the 1904 Act has been invoked against Michael Landers, does it mean that every other young person appearing in pantomime or shows, in theatres—the Gaiety Theatre or any other—will be forbidden to appear, or is the law to be rigidly enforced only against Michael Landers simply because his manager saw fit, in justice and fairness, to ask for an inquiry into the conduct of certain members of the Garda Síochána who, it was felt, were overstepping their duty.

"This has caused widespread uneasiness among the general public. One would imagine the Garda authorities have, at present, sufficient matters of great national importance on their hands such as unsolved murders and serious crimes of larceny, theft, treason etc to engage their attention instead of devoting all their energies to assembling the highest power at their disposal to trace a five-year-old boy around the country and rake up an Act of Parliament under which he can be prosecuted. This is wrong, unreasonable and very unfair. It is time the Minister for Justice told the Garda authorities to lay off this five-year-old boy. There is no sense or reason in it. This five-year-old boy is singing and providing entertainment, amusement, merriment, joy and happiness. He is providing excellent records and a fund of great amusement for music-lovers and song-lovers. The Garda authorities are going in full force to every hall in every part of Ireland in which this showband is billed.

"I did not raise this for the purpose of causing embarrassment to the commissioner of the Garda Siochana but I do say that he would be better occupied dealing with serious crime and leaving this boy alone. If the Minister says in his reply that this is a matter which is completely in the hands of the Garda authorities he should intervene and tell them that it is very unfair to dig up a 1904 Act to embarrass the parents of a most promising young boy and to prevent his attendance at functions with the showband with which he is associated. The Minister for Local Government will be replying on behalf of the Minister for Justice. I hope he will make it clear to us that if the Cruelty to Children Act, 1904 is to be invoked in the case of Michael Landers it will be invoked against all others and that he will not be picked out because of the dispute that took place with the Garda authorities in Westport.

"The Minister might also bear in mind that the parents of this boy are extremely well-known and popular. He is a member of a most talented and musical family and they are extremely embarrassed about the manner in which they have been hunted from place to place by the Garda authorities. When the prosecution took place under section 2 of the Prevention of Cruelty to Children Act, 1904, recently the most amusing thing was that the function which the boy was attending was being held for the purpose of raising funds for the prevention of cruelty to children. Despite that, the Gardai took legal action. It is most unreasonable that the commissioner of the Garda should circulate a memo to certain Garda stations. I know one was circulated to the superintendent in Castlebar, County Mayo. There was a query raised in it which I quoted at Question Time.

"A letter was sent from the commissioner's office to the superintendent in Castlebar. The Garda authorities in Dublin wrote that the writer noted from the files relating to the manager of this showband that the showband in question had a five-year-old singer. The commissioner asked: 'Do you think we have a case

An old picture *(top)* of a BNM turf-cutting machine with its crew in Edenderry in 1951 and *(left)* digging the drains in the early days of Bord na Mona's bog development were Sonny Burke (Galway), Tom Quirke (Wexford), Pat McGrath (Edenderry), Con Hayes (Limerick), and Pat O'Connor (Edenderry)

Larry Costelloe
and his wife Mary,
who met while
working for BNM

John Hayes
(Rathangan) who
came from Kilfinane,
Co Limerick, to work
in the Midlands with
BNM in the 1940s

Freshly cut machine turf in single rows
on a BNM bog near Rathangan, Co
Kildare... A turf footing as it should look
when properly constructed

interview the heavyweight champion of the world Floyd Patterson during a
visit to Rhode in the 1970s

The St Mary's
Junior School Band,
Edenderry *(above)* —
the drummer boy on
the extreme right is
me — and The Copper
Beech, Edenderry
(right)

Me with the late
Sir Henry Cooper
in London in the
1970s

Me checking out the
entertainment scene at
the age of 17

K
AR

spec-
will
the
tney
nro
day-
nth.
and
ong
Y's

Kevin Farrell, the Edenderry dance promoter, in a relaxed mood with the 'Gazette'

Georgie Fame   **Belgians Mob Herd**

Five-year-old Michael Landers *(above)* recordin his hit record 'If I Could B A Sailorman' at Eamonn Andrews Studios in Dubli and *(left)* Michael in a New Spotlight advert announcing details of his debut record

Record star at 5!

And now for a tour!

"MICHAEL LANDERS" (The youngest recording artist in the world)

Dear Friends,

If you would like to hear Michael's new record "If I could be a Sailorman" on R.T.E. drop a postcard to any of the following programmes: Pop Call, Hospital Requests, Overseas Requests, Rodgha Ceoili, Music on the Move, etc., etc. His record is still on sale in the shops.

As Michael is only five years old he cannot write too well, but he will appreciate if you write for him.

The words of his new record, or any information or enquiries can be had by writing to:

The Manager, "Michael Landers", Allenwood, Co. Kildare. Phone 60284 (Code 045).

A Michael Landers handout from the early 1970s *(left)*, Michael in the former Sunday Press newspaper *(above)* and Michael with pals at Kilcullen National School in The Daily Mirror *(below)*

Mike, 5, sets a singing record

(Clockwise from top left) Garda
Sgt Martin O'Neill, who was sent to
Edenderry in the '40s; Garda Sgt
John O'Reilly, a great community
garda; Judge Peter A Connell, who
told a defendant who shot up a
bank ATM: "You didn't do it in time.

Me presenting Ben Dolan with Best of Irish Award — Ben accepted it on behalf of his brother Joe following the singer's death in 2007 — and *(below)* Joe Dolan *(left)* and Dickie Rock *(right)*

The legend that is Johnny Logan *(left)* and *(below)* another legend, Brendan Grace

Greg Fox with his wife Debbie and children Cillian and Trevor *(right)* in their shop in Castledaly, Moate, and *(below)* Craig Helliwell *(left)*, the English prisoner who had sex in a cell with a female prison officer while in Mountjoy jail for drug-running, tells me his story

Ned Redmond and his wife Nancy at their home in Birmingham. Ned was incarcerated in Glencree and Daingean borstal schools

Fr Brendan Smyth appearing in court

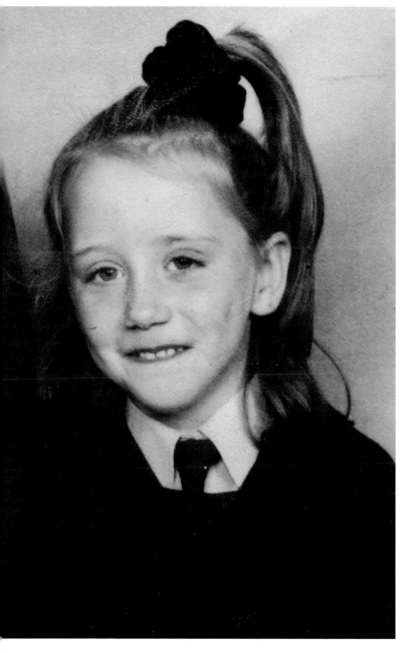

ary Maughan, who had been abducted on her way home from school
Westmeath. I found her later that night

Barry McGuigan after triumph, carried by trainer Jimmy Tibbs. Many years before this he fought at my club as a young teenager

AA All-Stars with Charlie Haughey *(second from left)*, me *(second from right)* and Eugene McGee *(right)* and *(below)* me at another crossroads in life.

(Above) Seamus Darby *(left)* and Tommy Doyle and *(right)* Seamus Darby of Offaly scores a last-minute goal past Kerry goalkeeper Charlie Nelligan, which denied Kerry five All-Ireland football titles in a row in 1982.

here?' They were looking for a case. They were trying to bolster up a case against a five-year-old boy. The Garda should not be asked to waste their time in this way. Their job is—and they are highly respected for it—to safeguard life and property. They should not have to waste time answering memos and watching newspapers to see if Michael Landers is appearing in some district.

"The Garda should carry out their duties impartially and there is nothing impartial about this. Why should this boy be singled out? It is wrong, unfair, unjust and unreasonable. The Minister should take the necessary steps with the Garda authorities to see to it that serious embarrassment is not caused to this little boy, to his parents, his manager and others. I hope the Minister will investigate this matter and consult with the Garda authorities to find why the Garda stations throughout the country have been alerted to watch out for a five-year-old boy. One would imagine that he was one of the most outrageous criminals this country has ever known. I am sure any broad-minded man would agree that it is wrong to have files in every Garda station in the country on a five-year-old boy because of his appearance at a musical event to sing a song. May we take it that from now on, since a court decision has been given in Bagenalstown, County Carlow, in relation to Michael Landers, that similar action will be taken in the case of all pantomimes and concerts?"

Minister for Local Government (Mr Molloy): *"I am not too sure why Deputy Flanagan was so anxious to bring this matter up on the adjournment today, since it was known in the House that the Minister for Justice is indisposed."*

Mr O.J. Flanagan: *"I am sorry to hear that."*

Mr Molloy: *"He was not here today to answer this question tabled by Deputy Flanagan, and it was answered on the Minister's behalf by the Minister for Finance. I got no notice that this matter was coming up but I can assure the Deputy that all he said will be brought to the notice of the Minister for Justice. At the same time,* following on what the Deputy said, I should like to put on the record again the reply which the Minister for Finance gave today on behalf of the Minister for Justice.

"The reply reads: As I have previously explained to the House on many occasions, the institution of criminal proceedings is a matter for the Garda Siochana acting where necessary in consultation with or on the directions of the law officers, and I have no responsibility in the matter.

"The Deputy can be absolutely assured that the Gardai got no direction from either the Minister or the Department to prosecute this boy. Indeed, it would have been quite improper for the Department or the Minister to give such a direction. The Gardai sought the directions of the law officers and they acted on the directions they got and, from what I know of the case, and from what Deputy Flanagan has said, I do not think the Gardai have any apology to make. Obviously there is a great difference between a young child singing in a commercial dance band, in the atmosphere of a dancehall, at a very late hour, and the appearance of children in pantomime or in a performance on a stage or in a theatre; their appearance on the stage is on a noncommercial or amateur basis, while this boy appeared professionally. I understand he was advertised as Michael Landers, the five-year-old wonder boy, and his band. I do not think I need say any more. I assure Deputy Flanagan that what he has said will be brought to the attention of the Minister for Justice."

CHAPTER 7

Seamus Darby, That Famous Goal And A Bottle Of Brandy

IT WAS in May 1982 that I attended an Offaly senior football championship match between Rhode and Daingean. Football in north Offaly was very strong at the time and both clubs would be represented at county level. I cannot recall much about the game itself other than the game ended in a draw and Seamus Darby scored a goal for Rhode that was so brilliant it would make his famous goal in that year's All-Ireland final look rather harmless.

There were no Tommy Doyles on the Daingean side but they did have sterling defenders and there would be no love lost between those two neighbours. Darby was about 40 yards out from the Daingean goal when he took a pass and immediately set off towards the goal. He got through at least three defenders before flattening the last one and sending what we would call a *"pile-driver"* to the top right corner of the Daingean net.

He was having the game of his life and looked the most dangerous forward I had seen in recent times, with the exception perhaps of Matt Connor. I stood there wondering how come this man was being ignored by the county selectors. When

I quizzed Seamus some time afterwards and put that very question to him he gave me the exact same reply. He didn't know either. By this period I had moved into journalism and was covering the odd local game for a local newspaper. After that particular game and subsequent games I asked in my reports why Seamus Darby was being ignored. Some readers agreed with me, but others disagreed, saying he was *"over the top"*, he was *"too heavy"* and, as journalist Vivienne Clarke said to me during one game, *"He's too pudgy."*

A few journalists, including myself, were chatting outside O'Connor Park after the championship replay between Rhode and Daingean when Offaly manager Eugene McGee approached us. *"Just want to tell you guys that Seamus Darby has been added to the senior panel, thanks."*

I was absolutely delighted and while no other journalist spoke or voiced an opinion, I knew that the way he was playing he wouldn't let me down. Of course the other journalists knew that he was my brother-in-law and they were not going to voice their opinions in front of me.

Seamus Darby made his comeback against Dublin in the Leinster final and ended the game on a personal tally of 1-3. I still find it amazing that even today few Offaly supporters ever recall that display. Do they even remember the fact that he played? Seamus pulled a hamstring before the semi-final and watched Offaly beat Galway from the sideline.

In July 1982 I was feeling off-colour and I was referred to the Midlands Regional Hospital at Tullamore by my GP for a colonoscopy. Seamus Darby drove me over from Edenderry for the appointment. The conversation from the time I got into the car was about football. I vividly remember as we approached Daingean, Seamus tapping me on the arm and saying, *"I'm going to tell you one thing. Offaly are going to win the All-Ireland this year."*

I didn't want to disappoint him but personally I couldn't see it. Kerry were on the crest of a wave and seemed to be improving all the time. I felt the Offaly players couldn't keep up the momentum. Some of those players had been around since the '70s. Players like Martin Furlong and Sean Lowry, and of course Seamus, were the remnants of the 1971/72 All-Ireland winning sides.

But I also appreciated that Eugene McGee would be aware of this. I believe that McGee's influence off the field was as big an asset as on the field. Through psychology, he kept them going. He nursed them individually, and listened to their personal problems. He was their football manager on the field and their agony aunt off it. I remember when McGee called a Press Night at their training grounds in Ballycommon prior to the All-Ireland final. The players had arrived and most were togged-out and warming up. The journalists were assembling and then McGee arrives, parks his car, gets out, opens the boot and takes out the cartons of milk and the sandwiches. He was an all-rounder. He did everything himself. I'm not sure if he actually made the tea and sandwiches that night but it wouldn't surprise me if he had.

It was around 9 o'clock on the night before the 1982 All-Ireland final and I was feeling the need for a pint of porter. I decided to call Seamus Darby to see if he would join me. Obviously I wasn't thinking too clearly. His wife answered the phone and said that Seamus was attending a players' meeting in Tullamore. When I told her I was just calling to see if he would go for a pint, she started to laugh. She wondered if I was really serious. The All-Ireland final was just hours away.

"Are you mad or what?" she said. *"Sure if he was seen out tonight he'd be shot."*

I said it was OK, that I'd see them all the next day, and I decided to stay put. Then at around 9.30pm Seamus phoned me. He repeated what his wife had said, and I explained that I just wasn't thinking right.

"Having said that I'd murder a drink, have you anything up there to drink?" Seamus asked.

I told him I had a bottle of brandy. He said he would get a bottle of lemonade and I asked him to get me two packets of cigarettes. Seamus was then living next door to Paddy McCormack, a legendary former Offaly player and then a publican in Edenderry. Soon Seamus was at my door with the lemonade and the cigs. We often laughed and wondered if punters in McCormack's pub that night admired Darby for buying a large bottle of lemonade and heading home. Being the good boy before the big occasion!

We chatted and he told us about their meeting in Tullamore and he was extremely psyched-up. Sitting on the edge of the couch in our sitting room he clenched his fist and said, *"By Jaysus if a Kerryman stood in front of me now I'd go through that fucking wall to get him."* This was before he got any brandy.

This wasn't any ordinary All-Ireland. This was the most talked about football final since the founding of the GAA. Kerry had four consecutive titles under their belt and they were going for the elusive Five-in-a-Row. This game had the nation on its toes. Thirty-one counties were on edge. Thirty-one counties favoured Kerry, but thirty-one counties were hoping for an Offaly win. We love the underdog, but very few outside Offaly gave the Midlanders a chance. In Kerry they were taking it so seriously. The players had become household names with individual stars being sought after for endorsements of all kinds of merchandise. One man had thousands and thousands of printed T-shirts stored at Shannon Airport ready to be flown to the United States that Sunday evening. The T-shirts celebrated the much-expected Five-in-a-Row. He was in for a killing! RTE Sports had a special programme in the can and they were ready to roll it soon after the great feat had been achieved. Then a local musical group in Kerry released a specially written song entitled *Five In A Row*. The chorus of the song went:

"Five in a row, five in a row,
It's hard to believe we won five in a row,
They came from the north, south east and the west,
But to Micko's machine, they were all second best."

But there was one verse that annoyed Offaly fans. It was the one that made little of Offaly's top forward and football legend, and the game's most modest man, Matt Connor. It read;

"In Offaly Matt Connor is a footballing star,
He scores goals and points from both near and far,
In Kerry we call him a Meteorite,
Cause his star rate had fallen by All-Ireland night."

Known as Matt *'The Trasher'* Connor, in a relatively short career he had chalked up a staggering 82 goals and 660 points before a car accident on Christmas Day 1984 left him paralysed, and robbed the nation of one the greatest players the game has ever seen.

If Kerry were a super team, and they were, Offaly were a unique side with just five households providing eleven players. There were five sets of brothers, and a set of first cousins. The team included brothers Sean, Brendan and Michael Lowry, Mick and Pat Fitzgerald, Matt and Richie Connor and their cousins, brothers Liam and Tomas. Then there were the Darby brothers, Stephen and Seamus. Leaving Seamus's goal aside, the Darbys created another record in that they were the first set of brothers to be brought on in an All-Ireland football final.

Eventually we opened the bottle of brandy and on the advice of our respective wives we started off by using a stainless steel egg cup as a measure. Apparently it is approximately the same measure as a pub optic. But after some time the egg cup fell on the ground and no-one bothered to pick it up. We managed to pour the rest without a measure or without spilling any. We polished off the bottle of brandy!

Then Seamus decided that he wanted to telephone the Parish Priest of Kilcock, Father John McWey. Affectionately known as Father Jack, he had been a curate in Edenderry from 1951 until 1975. Born in Slatey in County Carlow, he made Offaly his adopted county. He was also known to be a very lucky man and a man with a miraculous cure. During his 25-plus years in Edenderry he touched the lives of every family in the parish and performed what many believed were miracles. A lover of all things Gaelic, he was very involved in the local GAA club and played for Edenderry in his early days.

In 1964 when Offaly won their first ever All-Ireland minor football title, Father Jack was Chairman of the county minor board. When they won their first senior titles in 1971 and '72 he was Chairman of the senior county board.

Father Jack was delighted to hear from Seamus and they spoke about the game for about 10 minutes. As the conversation was ending and Father Jack was wishing him well, Seamus said, *"Of course Father, you do know I'm only a sub tomorrow"*, to which the late Father Jack replied, *"I know that Seamus, but you'll be brought in, and you'll score a goal. Goodnight now."*

I took my place in the Press Box in Croke Park that Sunday but even then I couldn't see Offaly toppling the champs. I had only spoken with two people during the previous week who said that they felt Offaly were going to win. They were the late Joe Dolan and Johnny Logan. To me neither of them knew anything about Gaelic football and were just saying it to please me!

Offaly were leading the All-Ireland champions at the interval and any ideas of a Kerry runaway victory had diminished. Offaly had more than matched the great champions for every minute. Kerry got on top in the second half and looked to have Offaly's measure, taking the lead as the rain started to fall. It really looked all over when Kerry were awarded a penalty and Mikey Sheehy stood over the ball. This would be the killer blow. This would lift Kerry to a higher plane and they'd probably "take-off" after that green flag was waved. Commentator Michael O'Hehir's words still ring in my ears: *"And Sheehy stands over that ball, five in a row they're bidding for..."* But the first of many eruptions followed when Offaly keeper Martin Furlong saved the shot and now it was Offaly who got the lift. But Kerry remained in front and looked home and dry with two points separating the sides with only minutes to go. Again, I can hear O'Hehir's golden voice, *"Is there a goal in this game?"* and he repeated, *"One wonders is there still a goal left in this game."* Did he know something?

Time was ticking away and few were leaving, except Kerry supporters trying to get back to the train. To them it was all wrapped-up and they were starting their celebrations. Just then Offaly were awarded a free from their own half-back line. Half the Offaly team had moved up. Few had even noticed that Offaly had replaced John Guinan with Seamus Darby. As Darby ran on the pitch McGee shouted after him to stay around the square in the hopes of getting a breaking ball. The free was taken by right half-back Pat Fitzgerald and caught by Richie Connor. He passed to his cousin Liam Connor who had moved up from his full-back position. Liam's delivery went high before dropping down between Seamus Darby and Kerry's great defender Tommy Doyle. Their bodies fused as they soared upwards and Darby's hands clenched the ball. On landing he swung on his right heel. Without further hesitation he let go with his left foot and the ball hit the back of the net. It was Seamus's only kick of the match and he had scored one of the most renowned All-Ireland goals in GAA history. Croker erupted. Offaly were now in front in the dying moments of the match. Could they hold out? Kerry attacked a few more times but failed to make the breakthrough. Three agonising minutes after the Darby goal the final whistle blew. Croke Park erupted again. Thirty-one counties celebrated. Darby's goal, one of the most famous GAA goals of all time, had robbed Kerry of the coveted Five-in-a-Row by just one point. Again I can hear O'Hehir's words, *"Offaly must now have won the most sensational of sensational finals."* They had indeed and victory was sweet. Like every Offaly supporter around the world that day I was so overcome with emotion that the tears flowed down my cheeks. All I could remember was that bottle of brandy I shared with Seamus a few hours earlier but most of all I could remember Father John McWey's parting words to Seamus and the priest's uncannily accurate prediction about him being brought onto the pitch and scoring a goal! The holy man had struck again!

CHAPTER 8

Laughter In Court

I WOULD love to have studied law but in my day it seemed like a closed shop, unless you had resources and connections. So the nearest I ever got to law was covering court cases as a journalist. Not a pleasant job if you are ordered to do it in your home territory and as we all know, it is easy to blame the messenger. But as Judge John Neilan once told me when I asked why he suggested that a convicted thug should have taken issue with the journalist, instead of with the garda, he replied, *"It goes with the territory."*

The judge had been told that the defendant was in breach of the Public Order Act and had given verbal abuse to the prosecuting garda. Judge Neilan asked the garda what the defendant's problem on the night was. When told by the garda that the defendant had been up at the previous court hearing and was upset about the report in the newspaper, the judge said he should have taken issue with the reporter. I was furious. Defendants in court cases were difficult enough to deal with, and that comment didn't help. Perhaps the judge meant to say that the defendant should have taken issue with the newspaper, but he said *"reporter"*. Having said that, the former District Judge John F Neilan was, in my opinion, one of the most efficient, fairest and most practical men to sit on the bench at that level. More of that later.

Another judge that impressed me greatly was the former Circuit Court Judge Kevin O'Higgins. In July 2008 he was nominated for appointment as a judge of the European Court of First Instance. He is descended from the O'Higgins family of Woodstown near Stradbally in County Laois, and has some distinguished family connections. He is related to Ireland's first Justice Minister, Kevin O'Higgins, assassinated in 1927, and also to former Presidential candidate Tom O'Higgins. Kevin O'Higgins is one of the longest serving judges in Ireland. I can vividly recall him asking two neighbouring farmers who appeared before him over a right of way to go outside and try to settle their differences. *"You are two grown men. You come in here today in a dispute over a piece of ground. You will spend days here costing you thousands of pounds and at the end of the day I will be asked to adjudicate on who is right and who is wrong. No matter which way it goes, you will leave here probably not talking to each other for the rest of your lives and it may carry on into succeeding generations. Is it worth it? I ask you again to go out and sort it out for both your sakes and your family sakes."*

Thirty minutes later their respective barristers told the court that the matter had been settled, to which Judge O'Higgins replied, *"I'm glad."*

I came across Judge Peter A Connellan when he was appointed to District Court area No 9, which at that time included courts in Counties Offaly, Westmeath and Longford. He was fond of the whiskey and owned The Silver Eel pub in Grange, near Strokestown in Roscommon. He could be very grumpy and set in his ways, but off the bench he could be good company and a great man for the yarns. He had such a hatred for banks and financial institutions that they must have celebrated when he retired from the bench. On the day he retired I happened to be in Edenderry District Court and afterwards I was invited by Garda Superintendent Gerry Murray to a few farewell drinks at Larkin's Bar. I had often wondered why he hated banks so much and I often wondered if it was something personal. I had been told that it was and that it resulted from an incident during a bank strike in the 1970s. But when I put this to him on the day he retired he denied it. *"My attitude with all of them (banks) was that if they get their arses burned they can sit on the blisters,"* he said.

At Tullamore District Court one day a local farmer came before Judge Connellan for discharging the two barrels of his shotgun into a Bank of Ireland ATM machine. The court heard how the farmer got a loan and soon afterwards the interest rates soared to 18 per cent. The poor man was badly caught and after selling some stock and paying off interest of around £60,000 the bank came back within months looking for the same again. The man lost it and drove into Tullamore before venting his anger on the ATM. Having heard the evidence in great detail, Judge Connellan looked down at the defendant and said, *"You didn't do it in time."*

Sitting in Daingean District Court on another occasion he lashed Credit Finance Bank. This was just about a year before they got into difficulties and were taken over by AIB. *"This Credit Finance Bank is beginning to get to me and particularly their Mullingar branch. They would pull you in off the street going by and fill your pockets with money and then take the roof from over your head if you can't pay it back. They give it out to people they should know damn well cannot pay it back. They are as far removed from brains as a dog from feathers."*

He had great sayings, often telling a witness, *"Get out of that witness box. Your teeth would fall out if you told the truth."*

Judge Connellan would not allow any defendant or solicitor to make excuses for not having car insurance. *"He either had it or he hadn't it. If he had it then show it to the guard, if he hadn't it, then I don't want to hear why he hadn't,"* he'd say, before convicting.

He was most reluctant to convict people for not having a television licence if there were children in the house. "*It is more important that these children can sit and enjoy television instead of being out robbin' and stealing around the town,*" he would tell TV inspectors, before dismissing the summons.

No judge in the history of the State ever made more national headlines for his outbursts than Judge John F Neilan, who retired from the bench in 2010. One newspaper journalist dubbed him *"Judge Dread"*. A native of Roscommon, he also served in District Court area No 9, before and after the boundary changes in 2007, a change that removed Offaly courts from the area.

No-one escaped the wrath of Judge John F Neilan, from superintendents to sergeants to ordinary Garda rank-and-file members of the force. He sorted out solicitors, court interpreters, RTE, the HSE, An Post, the Department of Justice, the Department of Trade and Enterprise, the Court Service; even the then Minister for Justice Michael McDowell didn't escape a lashing from Judge Neilan.

On his final day in Edenderry, the court burst into thunderous applause when he slated the Department of Trade and Enterprise. He was hearing a case where a businessman was before him on 19 charges of employing young people after 10pm. The court was told that the defendant was unaware of the regulation and had handed over his employment records in good faith to the Department.

Judge Neilan heard that the defendant had paid the workers above the rate. They were still in employment and appreciated the jobs. Judge Neilan asked if the young people were to be deprived of a chance of a few euro. *"Stand on street corners. Scratch your backside, take drugs, but whatever you do, don't go working,"* said the judge, as dozens of people in the courtroom stood up and gave him a standing ovation. *"Young people in gainful employment even an hour over time should not be penalised. It's far, far better to have them working than floating around or standing on street corners, insulting everyone who passes by."* He spoke of how, as a child, he had worked on the family farm late into the night when hay had to be saved. He said they didn't have health and safety regulations then. *"Now staff at Dunnes Stores and Tesco have to be told how to stack cornflakes. Next thing housewives and husbands will be taking courses in how to put away the boxes of cornflakes so they don't fall on their heads."*

He spoke of hearing a man on radio from Cappoquin in County Waterford talk of how regulations had destroyed its chicken production industry, because Irish producers had to work to stringent standards while imported "lumps of meat" bought for a cent in Thailand with no Government regulations carried the *"Guaranteed Irish"* label. *"I'd take those regulations and burn the lot and then I'd burn down the hen house if that's the way the Government and Western Europe want to work,"* he fumed. He added that one would think children were being treated as slaves, and before he asked why the incentive should be removed. *"I commend this businessman,"* said Judge Neilan dismissing all 19 charges, and concluding that many young people were only interested in drink and drugs and those who worked should not be penalised. Fresh charges were never brought against the defendant.

Judge Neilan was the first judge to order what was in effect a kind of electronic tagging of a defendant. At Edenderry District Court in May 2000 a former garda who was subsequently jailed for three years for making more than 3,000 nuisance phone calls to his former lover was the first citizen to be monitored by means of a mobile phone. The judge ordered that the State provide the defendant with a mobile set to take incoming calls only, which he was to carry with him at all times. He was also ordered to be ready to come to a Garda station within 15 minutes of being summoned to do so.

The humane side of Judge Neilan was always evident when he was dealing with hardship cases. There was an instance at a court sitting in the Midlands when an 18-year-old girl told him that she couldn't get a medical card.

The judge said he wanted the girl medically examined, adding that if he could, he would write her out a medical card in two seconds. *"I want you to go to the HSE office and say, 'I was sent by Judge Neilan and he wants me to have a medical card,'"* said the judge. Later in the day, Judge Neilan said he had received a letter from the HSE stating that the girl had been granted a medical card from that day.

Sitting at Edenderry court one day he questioned why an official of An Post was withdrawing a summons against a TV licence defaulter. When the official from An Post said the Postmaster was withdrawing it because the defendant had taken out a licence and paid the arrears, a furious Judge Neilan said the Postmaster was not going to run his court and that he (judge) and he alone would decide whether or not a summons issued would be withdrawn.

Judge Neilan can never be accused of discriminating when it comes to speaking his mind. He once crossed swords with the then Minister for Justice Michael McDowell when he said he would jail every drunk driver that came before him for at least one week. Minister McDowell made a statement in which he said that Judge Neilan didn't have such powers. This angered Judge Neilan who told the Minister to keep his nose out of matters concerning the judiciary. Some time later at Longford District Court when it was announced that Minister McDowell was coming to Longford to officially open the revamped court house, Judge Neilan retorted, *"If that fella thinks I'm going to stand on the steps of the court house to have me picture taken with him he's greatly mistaken."* And on being told at a court sitting that the defendant who breached the Public Order Act had served as a soldier, he commented, *"I wouldn't have him in Dad's Army".* Addressing bouncers from a night club where there had been a series of rows he remarked, *"Them bouncers wouldn't run a creche."*

During the foot-and-mouth crisis in 2001 he suggested that every pub, club and dance hall in Ireland be closed down until the *"all-clear"* was given. At Granard District Court he refused to allow the Longford County Council to remove their dance licence from the local hall saying it was an example of the dismantling of our heritage. A native of Roscommon, Judge Neilan once angered a woman from Clara, County Offaly, when he described her son at Kilbeggan District Court as *"an animal".* The woman ran from the body of the court and lunged at Judge Neilan before being removed by a large force of gardai. The court had to be halted during the melee.

He has also attacked the media over the years and in particular RTE. On being told at Mullingar Court that Marian Finucane had interviewed defendants, who were appearing on serious charges, on her radio programme, he asked, *"What business is it of Marian Finucane. Did she find them guilty?"* On another occasion he accused RTE of going and having *"afternoon tea"* with the family of a victim involved in a kidnapping. When he was told that a young man before him had been on his hands and knees on the main street of Ballymahon staring at the registration plate of the Garda car at 3am, he fumed, *"Listen here, me buck. If I ever see your snout in here again you'll be on your knees staring at the skirting board in the cell in St Pat's or Castlerea.*" When a Dublin-based medical doctor appeared before him at Edgeworthstown District Court for honking his horn at a driver who was driving within the limits the judge called him *"a bully boy".* He continually lashed the Health Service Executive, Midlands Area saying they *"didn't give a damn"* about accommodation of problem juveniles.

Over the years Judge Neilan has ordered several people to appear before him. One businessman was summoned to appear after the judge was told that the man's staff were not cooperating with a Garda investigation into an assault at a night club he owned. Judge Neilan can be extremely witty and was well known for such phrases as, *"Be here at the next court, Mister, with that compensation or bring your bags."* Hearing cases nearing Christmas time he would warn a defendant, *"The ball is in your court, Sir. It is up to you whether or not you want to have Christmas dinner at home or with the Governor of St Patrick's Institution."* He has also warned young rural defenders saying, *"You lads down here think you are tough. But I'll send you to St Patrick's and see how tough you are with the 'hard chaws' that are up there."* He told another young defendant, *"I'd sooner accept the garda's evidence than your evidence. He was sober on the night but you were full to the gills with porter."*

Most people feel that Judge John Neilan is a very fair judge who will always give a defendant a hearing. He always expresses concern for the elderly, particularly those who live alone, saying they are the people who made this country what it is today, and they have a right to be protected in their old age. He has also been praised for the tough manner in which he deals with public order offences. On an occasion in Tullamore District Court when a non-national passed some derogatory remark about the renowned Kennedy family in America, Judge Neilan pointed the finger at him and said, *"Listen here me buck. If it wasn't for John F Kennedy, God rest him, you'd still be staring through the barbed wire the far side of the Berlin Wall."*

He launched a scathing attack on an interpreter and told her that the defendant had more English than she did. It happened when a Lithuanian woman was appearing on a summons for not having a TV licence. Judge Neilan asked the defendant if she would be able to come back to court with a licence he adjourned the case to June 18. It emerged that the interpreter did not understand what the judge was saying but the defendant indicated that she understood. *"How am I supposed to convey what I need to convey? This woman has more English than you have,"* he told the interpreter. The judge went on to say that this was not the first time this had happened. He said he wondered how her employers could have employed this interpreter. *"If I don't get satisfaction then I'll retain my own interpreter,"* said Judge Neilan. He added that he had an excellent working relationship with interpreters. *"I would not like to see any of you offended,"* said Judge Neilan, who then presented the four interpreters in court with a copy of court protocol. *"It might help you,"* he said.

He has threatened to jail high-ranking gardai and stormed off the bench one day saying he would not hear any more cases in which this particular Garda officer was involved in. He accused another Garda officer of laughing at him, and when an inspector in a Midlands court told him he was not satisfied with him dismissing a case and that he'd bring it to a higher court he seethed with anger. *"Listen here Mister. I couldn't care less where you bring it, but you won't adopt that attitude in my court. Pack your bags now Sir, and get out of my court. This court stands adjourned until I see your backside going through them doors."*

He also gave his views on banks in his final days on the bench when told at Tullamore District Court that the defendant still owed the State €50,000 in fraudulent disability claims. He had been ordered to pay the State €400 a month but Judge Neilan heard he was only paying €200 a month because he was prioritising his debt of €210,000 to Bank of Ireland. Addressing the defendant's solicitor Judge Neilan said; *"Tell your client to tell the Bank of Ireland to take a flying jump. The taxpayers are paying billions to bail them out. I couldn't care less about the Bank of Ireland if they went floating down the Shannon in the morning. I've no interest in Bank of Ireland, or AIB, or any bank. I'd have more interest in turf banks."*

Judge Neilan retired in 2010 after 28 years on the bench. He dealt with his last case in Mullingar Court, and everyone was taken by surprise by the announcement that he was bowing out. The veteran judge indicated that he did not want to hear any tributes. *"I came in quietly and I'll go quietly,"* he said. And then he left the court smiling.

CHAPTER 9

Passing Of The Stars

THE death of any showband member always brings memories flooding back, and of course some deaths bring more memories than others. I was saddened by the death of the legendary Dermot O'Brien. It wasn't sudden. A lot of people knew that he was terminally ill. But that doesn't lessen the blow or the shock when it eventually happens. Dermot, who captained his native Louth to All-Ireland football glory in 1957, was one of the most accomplished accordion players this country ever produced. He will always be remembered for his single hit *The Merry Ploughboy* in the '60s. He got loads of television work and was one of the biggest attractions on the circuit in the '60s. It was Dermot who had played the backing track on Michael Landers' debut record, so I would have been friendly with him over the years.

Dermot O'Brien faded faster from the Irish music scene than one could imagine and he headed off to the US. On one of his trips home he told me that he had ended up playing in venues that at one stage in his career he would have refused to piss in. I also interviewed him a short time before he died. It was a conversation tinged with sadness and he told me how he had continually said to his wife that it wouldn't be the dragging and hauling of band equipment that would damage his health, but the smoke in the clubs and bars of New York. *"As the nights would progress in some New York bars the smoke was so thick you wouldn't be able to see the audience,"* he told me.

Dermot developed lung cancer. *"I'm getting the Louth Hall of Fame award next week, so they must think I haven't long left,"* he said to me jokingly. He passed away in 2007 and I was out of the country at the time and unable to attend his funeral. I still love to play the number he penned himself, *Dublin in 1962*.

Other entertainers that left us over the years affected me. There was Liam Gibson who died in 1997. Liam had come from Inchicore, Dublin, to join *The Houston Showband* in Edenderry. He was to go on to join Brian Coll and *The Buckaroos*, then Philomena Begley and her *Rambling Men*. He came to Edenderry in the mid-1970s and launched his own group. I had the pleasure of managing him. Then he joined Brendan Shine for a spell before returning a second time to the local scene. He died while performing in Banagher. He was an outstanding artist.

A member of Liam's group in the '70s was the talented Pat Cleary. He was one of the founder members of the *Agents Showband* in Edenderry. As I explained earlier, they later became *The Fairways* and were under the management of the then Release Records. Pat later joined *Larry and the Country Blue Boys* before going to London and going solo. He also gigged on the continent and came back to Ireland around 2001. He died tragically in 2009. A brilliant musician.

As earlier indicated, The Fairways were fronted by a singer called Gary Street (real name Joe Conway). He died in 2003. Another member of that band, Bobby Clarke, died in 2009. Billy Hopkins, who was part of the *Cluskey/Hopkins Guinness*

Jazz Band, died in 2010. A lovely guy and a talented bass player, he played with various combinations including *The Kings Showband*.

Mick Bryan died in a car crash in 1971. He was also a founder member of the Agents/Fairways. A talented songwriter and guitarist, he was a brother of Willie Bryan, the first Offaly man to lift the Sam Maguire Cup in 1971. Fran O'Toole was one of three members of *The Miami Showband* to be murdered by a loyalist killer squad while coming home from a Northern Ireland gig in 1975. *The Royal Showband*'s Tom Dunphy, who released Ireland's first ever showband record, *Katy Daly*, died in a car crash in County Leitrim while heading for a gig in 1975. Pat McGeegan (Pat McGuigan), another personal friend of mine, died in 1987. Pat was a gentleman and a great artist. Johnny Kelly, formerly of *The Capitol Showband*, also died in 1987 and is buried in his native Spiddal, County Galway. I had a lot of dealings with Johnny when he owned Ruby Records.

I had occasion to meet Donie Collins on one occasion. I dined with Donie, who fronted the *Donie Collins Showband*, in the former Eden Inn in Edenderry in the mid-1960s. I remember him leaving a sixpence tip on the table. Then some minutes later while still chatting to us he was fiddling with money in his hand when he discovered he had a three penny piece. He swapped his tip for the latter.

I heard Mick Delahunty performing a few times in the old Town Hall in Edenderry when he performed for the O'Brien UP Stores' annual dress dance. A professional to his finger tips. A native of Clonmel, County Tipperary, he died in 1992. I also had the pleasure of meeting Brose Walsh for an interview with his band in Mullingar's Greville Arms Hotel many years ago. He must have held the record for being the longest serving musician and band on the road. He launched his band in 1937. He passed away in 1995. A lovely man.

I never encountered Jack Ruane other than on the phone and we must have exchanged some details because his home address at 10 Morrison Terrace, Ballina is embedded in my memory. He died in 1997. I had never met Billy Brown of *The Freshmen* but his death in 1999 brought back memories of the good old days. The Freshmen were a brilliant outfit. I knew Gerry Walsh of *The Mighty Avons* very well. He went on to manage country singer John Hogan. Another member of the Avons passed away the following year — Brian Finlay. He was the funny man of the outfit. He also went into management and promotions. I had a pint with him in The Park House Hotel in Edgeworthstown in Longford a short period before he died. I was there covering a story for *The Star* and he came in with promotional posters.

Doc Carroll was a great artist that lasted longer than I would have thought he would. I played him in Edenderry's Town Hall in the '70s or perhaps earlier. Joe Dolan's death shocked us all. Apart from his playing for me in The Copper Beech in Edenderry (a venue he never managed to fill), as I indicated earlier, he played for me once a year, every Easter Saturday night, in Lawlor's ballroom in Naas.

I was very sorry to hear of the death of Brendan O'Brien in 2008. I had met him in the late 1980s or early 1990s when he was trying to launch a solo career. He looked a shadow of himself at the time and I felt so sorry for him. An amazing artist and I loved his performances.

Butch Moore was long left the Capitol Showband before I got to hear him "live". I first saw him when he fronted *The Kings Showband* after I booked them for a gig in Carbury, County Kildare. Many years later, while touring on a break from New York, I booked him for a solo slot in Daingean Town Hall in County Offaly. There was a very poor attendance and they threw pennies at him. It was one of the most pitiful sights I have seen. Here was the first man to represent his country in the Eurovision Song Contest, and this is what they thought of him now.

It was one of the first showband funerals I attended and the mourners filled St Canice's Church in his native Finglas, north Dublin, back in 2001. Butch had also battled with cancer for a short period, but Butch had told friends just weeks before his death that he'd beat it. It was not to be, and he finally succumbed to the dreaded disease at his Washington DC home. Butch Moore was already a household name before ever taking part in the Eurovision. As lead singer with the very successful and popular Capitol Showband he had built up a huge following of fans across the country and in parts of the UK. The band also featured the evergreen Paddy Cole and the Kelly brothers, Des and the late Johnny.

It was in 1965 that Butch represented Ireland in the Eurovision Song Contest in Naples, singing *Walking The Streets In The Rain*, written by 16-year-old Teresa O'Donnell from Suncroft, Co Kildare. The song finished sixth in the contest and became one of the most requested songs on RTE Radio, turning Butch Moore into a pop idol for young and old. Butch left The Capitol Showband towards the end of the '70s and spent one year on the road fronting The Kings Showband before emigrating to the US with ballad singer Maeve Mulvaney, who later became his wife. She was at his bedside when he passed away. They had been gigging as a duo from their home outside Washington, and topped the bill at every Irish fair and festival right across the US, attracting huge audiences.

Entertainers past and present were among the mourners that packed St Canice's Church for his Requiem Mass. They had come to comfort his wife Maeve and other members of the Moore family, but most of all they had come to say their final farewells to a colleague, a friend and an Irish showband legend.

Father Brian D'Arcy delivered a most emotional homily that had the huge congregation laughing and crying, but remembering. He described Butch as *"the greatest sex symbol ever"*. He also described Butch and The Capitol as the pioneers of the showband era. Father Brian said they had changed the face of Ireland, taking it from the priestly parish halls and paving the way for such groups as U2, Boyzone and Westlife who, he said, might not have happened otherwise. Father D'Arcy said that they started a business that eventually employed 10,000 people, an industry bigger than the meat industry back then. Fr Darcy chronicled the life and times of Butch from his school days in O'Connell School, to his time in the showband business and then the Eurovision, and to his success in the US as a duo with his wife Maeve.

"Butch Moore standing there shyly, handsomely, white suit, left foot forward, left hand beating time off his side was the greatest sex symbol ever," said Father Brian. He said it was lovely to see an ordinary man become such an amazing star. He also spoke of all the "firsts" that The Capitol had achieved.

• They were the first to record and release an album.

• They were the first to record an original number, *Fooling Time* written by Phil Coulter.

• They were the first showband to appear on Irish TV.

• They were the first showband to appear at The London Palladium, and the first to represent Ireland in the Eurovision Song Contest, watched by over 100 million viewers.

Having mentioned Butch's three biggest hit records, Fooling Time, Born To Be With You and of course his Eurovision song, Fr Brian concluded:

"Somehow or other I can see Butch walking up to God today and saying, 'no more fooling time, no more walking the streets in the rain, vocation achieved at last, I was born to be with you.'"

The chief celebrant of the Mass Fr Paul Thornton CC

welcomed Butch back to Finglas, the place where had been born and reared, and the place from where it all had started. Butch's colleagues from the Capitol, Paddy Cole (on clarinet) and Eamon Monaghan (on church organ) delivered a haunting rendition of the evergreen Eurovision hit *Walking The Streets In The Rain* during the Offertory of the Mass. Butch Moore's brother Des, a well-known session guitarist, played his last tribute before the final prayers of the Mass were recited.

Mourners included Johnny Logan, Joe Dolan, Brendan Grace, Ronnie Drew, Phil Coulter, Noel V Ginnitty, Eileen Reid, former Royal Showband manager Connie Lynch, Daniel O'Donnell's manager Sean Reilly, promoter Oliver Barry, Sean Dunphy, members of the Freshmen Showband, former leader of the Kings Showband Barry Cluskey, and the Hopkins brothers, Des and Billy, from the Guinness Jazz Band. As the remains were taken from St Canice's Church there was a cloud burst and the rains poured down. As we walked behind the hearse taking Butch (Seamus) Moore along the main street of his native Finglas for the last time, no-one knew who was crying... we were walking the streets in the rain.

****

It was around springtime 1986 and I was working in Portlaoise town when I got this bad pain in my chest. I was a bit concerned so I called to a local GP, a Dr Maguire, who examined me, briefly, then directed me to the hospital on the Dublin Road.

I was admitted without delay and I was wired-up within minutes. I spent about three weeks there having various tests. From there I ended up in the Blackrock Clinic before the late and legendary heart surgeon Dr Maurice Neligan. He passed me on to a Dr Brian Maurer at the Mater Private Hospital and he suggested an angiogram. I was over the moon after this test because not alone did it produce a clean bill of health but it revealed that I had an extra artery. I had been under quite an amount of stress at the time. I had just built a new house, became involved in the re-birth of a cabaret lounge and worked five to seven days a week at journalism. The medical experts eventually put my chest pains down to stress, and my friends who knew my lifestyle told everyone that I had suffered a 'Harp attack'.

As summer approached I had improved and was taking things a little easier. The local Lourdes Fund Committee, with whom I had been associated over many years, helping them raise funds, asked me if I'd like to join them on their annual pilgrimage to the holy shrine. I must admit that the chest pains had frightened me, and I thought that perhaps I should go and say a few prayers and make peace with my Maker at this very holy place.

I enjoyed the week and I remember one evening one of our party asked me if I had seen Monsignor James Horan from Knock, County Mayo. I didn't even know until then that he was in Lourdes. Monsignor Horan was renowned as the parish priest of Knock, with its pilgrimage centre. He had overseen the building of Knock Basilica, conducted a most remarkable campaign to bring an international airport to Knock, and was also credited with ensuring that Pope John Paul II visited Knock Shrine in 1979. My informant told me that he thought Monsignor Horan looked ill, and that when he saw him walking by the Lourdes grotto earlier that day the 75-year-old priest seemed to be holding onto the wall for support. I thought no more about it.

Friday morning dawned and I was down town picking up souvenirs. This was our last day in Lourdes. Then I heard the sad news that Monsignor Horan had passed away the previous night. Like all Irish pilgrims in Lourdes that day I was shocked. The death of any pilgrim is upsetting but this man was something of an icon. There was an air of gloom over the Irish pilgrims as they huddled in groups and particularly around the grotto area, talking about what a great man he had been and the great work he had done in providing an International Airport on what was then described as a "foggy bog" in Mayo.

I phoned the *Sunday World* and my good friend Sean Boyne was on the desk. He had just heard the news on radio. *"Guess where I am, Sean?"* I asked. *"I'm calling you from the Tara Hotel in Lourdes where Monsignor Horan died a few hours ago."*

At first he didn't believe me. He never thought I would be in Lourdes, above all places, and I hadn't told anyone I was going. But he was delighted when he discovered I was telling him the truth. *"Great, get what you can,"* he said.

I was fortunate to make it to the hospital morgue where the kindly pastor lay draped in the white vestments that had been handmade for him by the nuns of the Dominican Order in Drogheda for the 50th anniversary of his priesthood. He never did get to wear them while alive.

Unfortunately, time was ticking away and I had only a couple of hours to spare. Our group were about to leave for the airport. I spoke with people at The Tara Hotel. Coincidentally, Monsignor Horan's cousin Father Pat Mulroe was there with a group from Shrewsbury in England and he presided at prayers over the remains on the great man. I spoke to Father Pat just before I left for the airport. The Monsignor's four sisters were also in the hotel but I didn't get to see them. Father Pat and Father John Porter from Knock were preparing to say the Requiem Mass at the century-old Seven Dolours Church that evening. One man I did meet before departing for Dublin was Tom Neary, who was chief steward at Knock and a close friend of Monsignor Horan. Over a coffee he told me how Monsignor Horan had joined the party the previous night. Other pilgrims remembered him singing *Kevin Barry* while sipping a small glass of beer at the bar of the Tara Hotel overlooking the River Gave. One of our group recalled seeing Monsignor Horan the previous evening. *"He was wearing a black short-sleeved shirt and seemed very, very weak. He carried a small set of brown Rosary beads and when he reached the spot at the grotto just underneath the statue of Our Lady, he paused and kissed the rock,"* the man told me.

The following Monday his body was flown into Knock International Airport. It was a sad but fitting tribute to the most renowned parish priest in Ireland, who had founded this great facility for his flock, against all the odds.

It was a sad end to my first trip to Lourdes, yet I was glad to be the only Irish journalist there and I was conscious that Monsignor Horan always appreciated the support given him by the *Sunday World* during his long campaign to build his airport. He had sent several letters of thanks to the then Deputy Editor, Bill Stuart.

Early in 2011 I attended a musical based on the life and achievements of the great man in the Royal Theatre in Castlebar. Entitled *On a Wing and A Prayer*, it was presented and produced locally by members of his own flock, the people who knew and loved him. For an amateur production it was just brilliant.

CHAPTER 10

A Killer Brought To Book

THE murder of Phyllis Murphy (23) back in December 1979 is one crime that will always remain embedded in my memory. It was the very first murder case I reported on as a journalist. Little did I realise that 23 years later I would be sitting shoulder to shoulder beside her killer as the guilty verdict was delivered in the Central Criminal Court in Dublin. One of the gardai involved in the case, Pat Donlon, who liaised with the Murphy family over the decades, was serving out his last days in the force as a detective when Phyllis Murphy's neighbour, John Crerar, was found guilty and sentenced to life imprisonment.

As a young reporter back then I was intrigued by the manner in which such crimes were investigated. I was lucky in that I got a sort of first-hand insight. Within 24 hours of Phyllis Murphy going missing, search parties had been organised. Hundreds of local people and organisations combed fields and ditches around her native Kildare town as well as the vast Curragh plains. But when the body was found, everything changed. The search for a missing girl had now been transformed into a murder investigation. Scores of gardai were assigned to the case. Their task included house-to-house calls, taking statements, attending daily conferences, comparing notes, checking and re-checking every single line of every statement. Dozens of people were calling to Kildare Garda Station with pieces of information while others were calling to make statements, and supply blood specimens.

In a town where horse racing and Gaelic football make for most of the conversations in the local hostelries, the nightly discussions were now all about Phyllis Murphy. The conversations were eerie in a sense, for those who knew Phyllis were all subscribing to the theory that she would not get into a car with a person that she didn't know. It was always accepted that Phyllis knew her killer. It was felt that her murderer was not far away and maybe he was sitting at the other end of the bar counter. At one stage people were actually dropping names of those they believed to be the prime suspect. They seemed to think it was just a matter of picking him up. The brutal murder had a devastating effect on teenage girls and women all over the country, but particularly in the Kildare area. Young girls who worked in local factories were insisting on being escorted to and from work by boyfriends, brothers or parents. Attendance figures at cinemas and dance halls dropped dramatically. The social scene in the Kildare, Newbridge and Naas areas almost ground to a halt. Some local girls got totally carried away with all the publicity that the murder had attracted on the area, and gardai investigating the brutal killing of the 23-year-old Kildare girl were hampered by numerous bogus calls, or calls based on imagined threats. Several girls claimed they were attacked while others claimed that they had been approached by men in cars inviting them to go for a drive.

Working for the *Sunday World*, it was a cold, dark evening in January 1980 when I attempted to interview the colleagues of Phyllis Murphy as they left Curragh Knitwear, the factory in Newbridge where Phyllis had been employed only weeks earlier. They were too terrified to talk as they scurried to waiting cars and even motorbikes to get a lift home. None of them, particularly young women, were talking to strangers. At Killina in Carbury, a 16-year-old schoolgirl reported that she had been approached by a masked man while walking near her home. Detective Superintendent John Courtney, who was leading the Garda investigation, said almost immediately that they were not taking the girl's claims seriously. A pregnant woman in the Brannockstown area of Kildare claimed she was attacked by a man as she walked towards her home with a bucket of water from a roadside pump. She told gardai that the man jumped out of a car and pulled her skirt off. She claimed that she fought him off by throwing the bucket of water over him and lunging at him with her torch. Ten gardai were assigned to investigate her claims, but following four days of intensive inquiries they discovered that the incident never took place. Superintendent Courtney said at the time that he was very annoyed by the amount of time being wasted by such claims. His members had by this stage interviewed more than 16,000 people.

On Friday, January 18, 1980, I was the only reporter present when the body of Phyllis Murphy was found in the Wicklow Mountains. It was pelting snow as I parked my car and walked almost to the spot where the body had been located. The immediate area had just been sealed off, and one of the gardai on duty informed me that what lay just yards away *"was not a pretty sight"*. As darkness descended I made my way back towards the village of Hollywood. Through the huge white flakes of snow I could see the blue flashing lights of the Naas Ambulance as it made its way up through the Wicklow Gap to collect the frozen body of the young woman from the snow-covered mountain. It was a day I will always remember. Ten years later I had an exclusive interview with Barbara Turner, the eldest sister of Phyllis Murphy. She spoke of how her family was still grieving, and how their father had passed on four years previously, and died a broken man because no-one had ever been brought to justice. On that occasion Barbara Turner, with uncanny foresight, stated, *"We know nothing will ever bring Phyllis back to us, but we are still hoping that whoever murdered her will be caught. He is still free, and we are still convinced that he knows us and we know him."*

On Saturday December 22, 1979, Phyllis Murphy had gone shopping in Newbridge for Christmas presents for her father, nieces, nephews and friends. She also visited a hair salon in the town and shopped in the arcade, purchasing some goods for herself, including a pair of knee-length boots. Before leaving Newbridge for her native Kildare, just five miles across the Curragh plains, Phyllis called to see her best friend Barbara Luker who lived in one of the cottages opposite the Keadeen Hotel. Barbara was not at home when Phyllis called, but Barbara's mum, the late Margaret Luker left Phyllis to the gate and watched as she walked to the bus stop to get the 6.30pm bus to Kildare. The bus stop was just yards away, and they said their farewells. Phyllis was carrying a weekend case and some bags of shopping.

Phyllis would not have been unduly disappointed about not finding Barbara at home as the two friends had an arrangement to meet anyway later that evening in Kildare. But when Barbara arrived in Kildare, there was no sign of Phyllis at the spot they were to meet, the bus stop at the Jet filling station. Barbara immediately knew something was wrong, because Phyllis was so reliable in keeping appointments. Barbara then went to the Derby House Hotel where both of them had planned to socialise that night. Inside the venue she met Patrick Murphy, a brother of Phyllis. They both agreed something was wrong.

They decided to tell her sisters, but not her father, for fear of upsetting him. Barbara later got a lift home to Newbridge.

The following day, Sunday, Phyllis Murphy was reported missing to the Gardai. It was also on that day that a 13-year-old boy, Ronan Fitzpatrick, joined his dad, as he did on most Sunday evenings, for a stroll on the edge of the Curragh. Ronan's mum had dropped them off on the outskirts of Kildare town at a place known locally as 'Colgan's Cut'. It was about 3.30pm. After walking a short distance Ronan saw a pair of knee-length boots on the ground. They were known then as 'cowboy boots'. The boots looked new. Neither Ronan nor his dad knew what to do with the boots but they ended up taking them home. They also found a baby's red cardigan, some Christmas wrapping paper, and a Christmas gift card with the words, *'To Father from Phyllis'*. On hearing that a girl had been reported missing, the Fitzpatricks took the items they found to the home of a local garda whom they knew personally. By now, it seemed that half the population of Kildare was out searching for Phyllis Murphy.

On December 29, one of those involved in the search, Louis O'Carroll, found a pair of mittens, also at Colgan's Cut. Inside one of the mittens were six ten-pence pieces. Gardai believe that the 60p was for Phyllis Murphy's bus fare home from Newbridge to Kildare town. Another significant find was made by John Mackey. This was a grey belt from Phyllis Murphy's coat. Gardai tried to establish if it had been removed in a struggle inside a vehicle, or grabbed by an assailant, and came loose from her coat as she tried to escape. The previous day, a young man named John O'Neill had found a weekend case as well as some Christmas presents under briars at Harristown Estate in Brannockstown on the road to Ballymore Eustace. Investigating gardai had now established that a car had been used in the abduction of Phyllis and that the direction it appeared to have taken was towards the Wicklow Mountains.

On January 18, 1980, gardai from Naas were assigned to conduct a search from Turlough Hill back towards the west Wicklow village of Hollywood. Having started at 9.15am, the exhaustive search was to include the land on both sides of the bleak mountain road, and at least 50 feet deep into the forest. It was past midday when Garda John McManus observed what appeared to be a pair of feet protruding from under some brambles approximately 10 yards in from the road in the townland of Ballingee.

Further investigations revealed the naked body of a female, lying prostrate with both arms above the head. It was a gruesome and terrifying sight. Within hours it was firmly established that it was the body of Phyllis Murphy. State pathologist Dr John Harbison was called in to carry out a preliminary examination before the body was removed to Naas General Hospital, where Dr Harbison conducted a post-mortem examination. It was established that Phyllis had been brutally raped and strangled before her body was dumped on the remote, isolated mountainside. The search was now on for the killer of Phyllis Murphy and it was to last for over 19 years.

Garda Finbar McPaul took care to ensure the safe filing away of an envelope delivered to Kildare Garda Station on December 20, 1988. The brown envelope was brought there from Naas Garda Station by Detective Garda Christy Sheridan as gardai at Naas were sorting out files on the occasion of their moving to their new station in the county capital. The envelope contained confidential documents, statements and, most important of all, semen samples taken from the body of Phyllis Murphy, who was murdered more than seven years earlier. After taking possession of that envelope, Garda McPaul put it away where he knew it would be safe, and where it could be found without delay should the need ever arise.

The envelope had been lying untouched at the old Garda

station in Naas for seven years having being returned there on July 22, 1981, from the Garda Forensic Laboratory in the Phoenix Park. After being sent to Kildare, it was to remain in the Garda station there until July 1997 when Detective Garda Brendan McArdle, of the Ballistics Section at Garda Headquarters, decided that with the amazing advances in DNA testing it might now be possible to solve old crimes.

Gardai in every station in the nation were requested to check on unsolved crime files, and when it came to Kildare, the Phyllis Murphy murder was undoubtedly number one on the list of cases deemed suitable for further inquiry. The Murphy samples were examined by Maureen Smyth of the Forensic Science Laboratory, and then Detective Garda McArdle brought the samples to a specialist laboratory in Oxfordshire, run by Selmark Diagnostics Ltd, for further analysis.

There was great excitement when the laboratory reported back that they had been successful in taking a blood sample from the semen found inside the body of Ms Murphy. The blood was then placed on a "stain card" and the laboratory confirmed that they could now clearly identify the blood and match it with that of the killer. The laboratory then ordered samples of blood taken from suspects at the time. But the initial excitement led to frustration when the first eight samples, and a further six samples proved negative. Garda chiefs were also calling a halt to any more samples being sent to England because of the enormous cost of carrying out the analysis. But gardai who had been involved in the case pleaded that they be allowed to send the remainder of the samples.

One of those samples was that of John Crerar. As one garda put it at the time of his arrest, "*He was always in the net, but to be honest he was not in our top 30 suspects.*" Crerar was one of seven men who presented themselves at Kildare Garda Station on March 6, 1980. The blood sample was taken by the then local

GP, Dr Bains. More than 19 years later, on February 16, 1999, Crerar's sample was sent to the laboratory in Selmark. Some weeks later there was Garda euphoria when it was confirmed Crerar's sample had matched the blood sample taken from the semen found on the body of Phyllis Murphy. After almost 20 years they believed they had their man, and John Crerar, a near neighbour of Phyllis Murphy, was arrested in a dawn swoop on July 13, 1999. He appeared the following day at Naas District Court before the late District Court Justice Thomas Ballagh.

While Garda McPaul was minding that envelope containing the crucial samples, his colleague in Kildare town Garda Pat Donlon, later promoted to Detective, who was one of the first gardai involved in the murder investigation, continued to liaise with the grieving Murphy family. He was providing whatever solace he could and reassuring them at all times that the file was still open and that one day a breakthrough might be made. When John Crerar was charged with the Murphy murder in 1999, Detective Garda Donlon was given the mammoth task of contacting potential witnesses, some of whom were now living in Australia, Germany, Amsterdam, parts of the UK and in various parts of Ireland. Ninety-eight witnesses were eventually summoned to the trial at Dublin's Central Criminal Court. When the guilty verdict on John Crerar was finally announced at the court on October 31 2002, Detective Garda Pat Donlon was the only member of the original investigating team still serving. He had just weeks left as a member of An Garda Siochana.

The court was crowded and the sense of drama was intense as the jury returned its verdict. I was among a large number of journalists present. There was not much space for the reporters, and I found myself sitting right beside Crerar as he was found guilty. I had covered the disappearance of Phyllis Murphy all those years before, and was now present to see the killer brought to book. It was a terrible crime, and as a journalist it was good to be there, to see justice done at last.

When Phyllis Murphy was murdered in December 1979, a 31-year-old Carlow man wondered if he might be related. Before changing his name by deed poll, Paul Delaney's name was Murphy and he was also aware that his birth mother had been a young Kildare woman. Now 23 years later he was to discover that Phyllis Murphy was in fact his half-sister.

For three-and-a-half weeks in 2002, Paul Delaney attended the trial of the man accused of murdering Phyllis, the sister he never knew. As the verdict was announced tears streamed down the cheeks of the 54-year-old father-of-two, who was so relieved that at last someone had been convicted of her murder, although he could still feel the pain of never knowing her.

Paul's mother was only 20 when she gave birth to him in the 1940s in a home in Roscrea. He has had it confirmed through a sister of his mother, who then lived in England, that he spent just one night with his mum in Kildare town before being fostered by a couple in Carlow. His foster parents John and Nora Delaney were very kind to him and gave him a good upbringing. His adoption was arranged through a priest friend, but it was never formalised or recorded. This created major headaches when he came to look for his natural family. However, a social worker from Athy traced his roots and discovered that his mother had died at the age of 42. Her maiden name had been Murphy, and she had married a Michael Murphy.

Before meeting his long-lost family, he visited Phyllis's grave in Kildare and laid a wreath of fresh flowers. His wife Breda recalls that this was a very moving moment for Paul, who had often talked about the brutal murder back in 1979, and had wondered if they might be related. When Paul and his wife met the Murphy family for the first time, they presented him with a card that read, *"Welcome Paul, we were shocked and delighted when we heard we had another member of the family. We all welcome you and your family to the Murphy clan."*

Paul said that the trial, while sad and very trying, had brought them all even closer. Phyllis Murphy's sister Barbara said the family were very upset when John Crerar lodged an appeal against his life sentence for the murder. She told me at the time, *"Never a day goes by that we don't talk about Phyllis. We will never ever see her again. John Crerar should accept his punishment."* He later withdrew his appeal.

CHAPTER 11

Little Girl Abducted

IT HAD been one of those weeks when any journalist would feel he had covered enough tragedies to do him a lifetime. To say that we reporters become immune to tragedy would be untrue. Perhaps through the very nature of our job we try to distance ourselves from tragedies without being conscious of the fact, or feeling that we are acting in a callous manner. The second weekend in November 2001 had its share of tragedies and I had just returned from spending two days in County Kilkenny after reporting on a particularly bad one.

The following day I was coming near the end of an ordinary day at the office when news broke that a little eight-year-old girl had been abducted while on her way home from school in the Midlands. First reports indicated that she had been dragged screaming into a dark green car by a man, and that the car sped off into the night in a remote area. All sorts of strange things ran through my mind as I left the *Irish Daily Star* office on that dark, dank November evening. What could be happening to this little girl right now? Was she still alive? Who could be so cruel and so sick as to snatch one so young, so innocent? I had been on difficult assignments before. I had knocked on the door of families torn apart by tragedy. Some stand out more than others. One particular one will stay with me forever. That was when a man had lost his wife and seven children in a fire. How do you approach him? What do you say to him? Or what do you say to grandparents whose daughter and two little grandchildren have been hacked to death by their own father? Yes, I'd been through it all in my 25 years as a journalist, but experiences of the past never seem to act as a cushion for the present or the future. I was desperately trying to detach myself emotionally from this latest story as I sped down the M4 towards Enfield. But it just wasn't possible. A parent's love for a child is one of the most powerful forces imaginable. As a father of three (although mine are grown up) I was placing myself in the shoes of the parents of little Mary Maughan in Moate, County Westmeath.

As a parent, if your child is away from the house, if the key doesn't turn in the door at the hour you expect it, your mind starts working overtime. Unspeakable terrors spring out of the dark and haunt your thoughts until that loved one is safely home. I couldn't even start to imagine how a mum or dad would feel, knowing a man had bundled their little girl, screaming, into a car and sped off into the evening gloom. As I had rushed out the door of the newsroom that evening the words of a shocked colleague rang over and over in my ears. *"And to think that I voted to abolish capital punishment,"* he said.

That journey from the newspaper office in Terenure, Dublin, to Moate lasted over two hours but it felt like 10. The nightmare I had often feared had now become a reality for the Maughan family.

The journey seemed endless. On my way to a town or village to cover a story I always start thinking about who I might know there. From my days in journalism, and before that in showbiz, I always seem to know someone who knows someone. It's a great help when you are arriving in a strange town. It doesn't happen by either accident or luck either. You build up your contacts. You appreciate people's help and assistance, and more importantly, you must show it. Some journalists I know are great at 'bullshitting' punters about how great they are. Then the next day after the story appears the person who helped them out is well forgotten. When some person down the country helps me out I take time the next day to drop them a personal note saying 'thanks'. It costs damn all, but it means a lot.

In Moate, I knew Tom Allen, better known as singer T.R. Dallas. Then of course there was Liam Claffey. I had done a story on Liam when he was just a teenager. Liam had donated a kidney to his older brother, the late Kieran Claffey, that wonderful Offaly footballer. I also knew that if Liam, who runs The Auld Shebeen pub, was around that I wouldn't be stuck for a late jar either. After all the drama of that night I did end up in his pub. I was glad to borrow his mobile phone while he charged mine for me, and pulled pints until very late.

Despite all my thinking about the job on hand as I sped towards Moate that evening I didn't know what I might say as I pulled up outside the Maughan family's door in the tiny townland of Knockdomney, one mile from Moate.

Understandably there was sheer pandemonium inside that house. The entire family, including the child's grand-mother, were praying aloud and calling on every saint I'd ever heard of to help find Mary. Kathleen Maughan sobbed uncontrollably as she told me how Mary had been so looking forward to Christmas and to receiving her First Communion the following year. Mary's father Paul Joyce said that Mary was so innocent. She was one who could see no wrong in anyone. He said he was praying and hoping that Mary would not be harmed or interfered with in any way. I left the house just before 9pm and said I would call and interview some of their neighbours.

Mary's 14-year-old cousin Willie Doran volunteered to come with me. He knew every house in the area, and for me time was of the essence. As I was about to call at the first house I received a call on my mobile phone from Stephen O'Brien at *The Star* news desk who was looking for an update on the story. By the time we had finished our conversation I had driven past the house where I had intended on calling, so I made a U-turn. Just as I was executing that manoeuvre I noticed a little girl running towards the front passenger door of my car. As she knocked on it, young Willie screamed, *"It's Mary, Jesus it's Mary."* Opening the door he grabbed her and pulled her into my car. Cold, trembling, shaking and sobbing, Mary Maughan held my hand as she told me how she had escaped from her abductor when he got out of his car to go to the toilet. I will never, ever forget that moment. But I can honestly say that my one and only priority was to re-unite that little girl with her parents.

As we sped back towards her home we came upon a Garda checkpoint and that was when I handed Mary over to the Gardai. I continued to drive to the Maughan home and breaking the news was another moment I will always cherish. It took almost 20 seconds before her parents really grasped the news that Mary was safe. A near tragedy had turned to triumph before my very eyes as the local Parish Priest led all and sundry in a prayer of thanksgiving. I know that I will never again witness an evening like it. The following morning I was featured on RTE's Morning Ireland, 2FM with Gerry Ryan, RTE and TV3 television and 14 local radio stations. It might be the dream of many a journalist to become the hero of a story. But I will never look at it like that. Mary Maughan had someone's prayer, and I just happened to be the one who was in the right place at the right time. For that and for Mary's safe return I will be always grateful.

Just six months later, almost to the day, a ten-year-old girl from Kilbeggan, just up the road from Moate in County Westmeath was abducted when running an errand for her mum to the local shop. She too, like Mary Maughan, was bundled into a car and driven away at high speed. She was held for four hours during which time she was sexually assaulted before being released.

Some hours later at around midnight, a car failed to stop at a Garda checkpoint in the area. The car registration was noted and it brought gardai to a house at Cappincur near Tullamore, to the home of a 34-year-old single man Kevin Healion. They seized his car, a computer and a digital camera. Mr Healion was later charged with the abduction of both girls. He subsequently pleaded guilty. On October 20, 2004, Kevin Healion received two 10-year sentences, to run concurrently, with the last year suspended.

****

It was in June 2003 that I got a story about a young prisoner being engaged in sex acts with a female prison officer at Mountjoy Prison in Dublin. When the *Irish Daily Star* carried the story under the heading '*Sex In The Cell*', there was a furious reaction from the Irish Prison Service. Members of the Prison Officers Association were equally furious as within hours of the newspaper hitting the streets they issued a strong denial statement and called on *The Star* to withdraw the story.

I was told that the young prisoner was whisked away so fast from Mountjoy that he didn't get time to get all his stuff together. The female officer was suspended and then she resigned. I genuinely felt sorry for the prisoner concerned, Craig Helliwell, and so I decided to visit him at the Midlands Prison in Portlaoise. I was refused admission. I was quizzed by an officer, before being told that although Mr Helliwell had not refused to see me, I wasn't on his 'visitors' list' and would have to apply in writing for permission to visit him. As I left the prison that morning I vowed that one day I would speak with Craig Helliwell. But then I forgot the whole story.

Four years passed and one morning when I arrived at the *Star* office, one of my colleagues who had been on the late shift the previous night said that a Craig someone or other had called from England and he wanted to talk to me about his time in Mountjoy jail. I was delighted. I immediately made contact with Craig Helliwell and I agreed to fly over to meet him and get the true story of what had taken place behind the bars and the walls of Mountjoy as well as at the Midlands Prison in Portlaoise.

Craig Helliwell (27), from Barnsley in England, sipped his pint of lager in an English pub on a Saturday morning. We were both making small talk and it was obvious that we were both trying to size each other up. He was wearing a blue track suit, and seemed very relaxed. Breaking into a grin he stared at me and blurted, *"I'm told that our sex act rocked the Prison Service."*

Craig Helliwell and another young man were arrested at Dublin Airport in 2001 and found to have hash valued at €200,000 each in their possession. Helliwell spent eight months on remand at Cloverhill Prison in Clondalkin, Dublin before being sentenced to six years. He was to spend the first 18 months in Mountjoy until a female prison officer whom I shall call Michelle (not her real name) fell in love with the young Englishman.

I gave Craig an open floor during his chat with me, and

I told him I wanted the story from beginning to end, and I promised not to interrupt him. This is the story that Craig recounted to me in my bedroom at the Hotel Ibis in Manchester:

"It was pointed out to me by inmates that she (Michelle) was looking at me. I thought they were winding me up. I kept it at the back of my mind. I was not personally attracted to her. She was not my type, not at all. I was walking down the stairs one day and she gave me a nudge with her elbow. I thought at the time that it was a male officer. I looked back and she was smiling at me. A couple of days later I was coming in from playing football. I had a little bit of water left in a coke can. I was running upstairs and I pretended to trip and threw the water in her face. I knew if she put me on a P19, (that's a report for a misdemeanour), I'll know I'm not in, if she doesn't, I have a chance. A few days later she said, 'Why did you throw that water in my face?' I said, 'You didn't put me on a P19, did you?' We started talking from then. That's really how it all started. She used bring me a couple of packages of chewing gum. You cannot buy chewing gum in Mountjoy. Then she brought me in a couple of CDs and a couple of tapes. Missy Elliott and dance CDs. Later in the relationship she bought me a watch. A sports watch that they (the authorities) confiscated the day that I was transferred.

"It all started off when she said to me one day, 'What are you doing for Christmas?' I said, 'I'm doing nothing, why?' I added, 'Give me your number and I'll give you a ring.' She said, 'No, give me your number.' The first night she gave me a call about 10.45 or 11 o'clock. I was in bed and she said she in was in bed. She said she was at home. We were talking for three to four hours. I think she was really into me. The first three hours was about her family and my family and why I got caught up in all this trouble. Then it got to a sexual nature. I asked her what she was wearing and she asked what I was wearing. She took her clothes *off and started to play with herself, the whole lot. I was doing the same thing. She would ring three or four times a week for three hours at a time. She sounded excited and she said she reached an orgasm."*

(According to Craig, the relationship then developed from phone sex into physical encounters in his cell).

"I climaxed twice when she was masturbating me. I'd have my top off, and I always wore shorts, so she'd just pull them down. I would ejaculate into her hand and she would wipe her hand in my tee-shirt or my shorts. She was always in and out of my cell. She was anxious for sex but afraid. We just had foreplay. I felt her breasts under her clothes. She was more paranoid than nervous. I wasn't attracted to her. She was like a double-decker bus, and from behind she looked like a Fiat Punto. If I seen her in a pub I wouldn't even talk to her. For me it was just anything to get me through my years. I was lonely, and afraid to refuse her, anything to just get me through. I told a few of the lads in the prison about what was going on. I was caught in the act by a few lads. I can remember an officer, (we'll call him X). I think he had a part in us being reported. Michelle was in my cell masturbating me this day. She looked down and Mr X was looking up. I'm 99.9 per cent sure it was Mr X. I'd put my life on it. She pulled my shorts up. We were just inside the cell door.

"When I was transferred to the Midlands Prison a few of the lads contacted me from Mountjoy and said it was Mr X that grassed me up. The day I was transferred I got a cell search that morning. They usually lasted two to three minutes. This one lasted 35 minutes. I had loads of English football posters on the wall. They took them all down. They took all my clothes and threw them in a corner, and messed up my cell. They found nothing except the watch that Michelle bought me. At that time I used to work in the laundry. I told the officers I got it from one of the lads. It was an expensive one. At 12.30pm that day Michelle came to my

cell and said, 'I've got bad news. You are being transferred to the Midlands Prison in Portlaoise'.

"I knew straight away what it was for. She said that I should go and ask the chief if I could stay. She said I had to plead my case to the chief. She said, 'Please do it for me'. I pleaded my case with Chief Officer Hughes, but he refused. Michelle was on the mini-bus when I went out. She reached over to me and said, 'Put my name down on your phone card', and then she got off the bus. It was a Friday. I put her name on my phone card using a pseudonym. I used to call her from the Midlands Prison while she was working in Mountjoy. Two high-ranking officers pulled me into an office one day. They asked, 'Who have you got down on your phone card?' I said family and friends. They looked at each other and said, 'Don't fuck with us'. They said, 'You're phoning Michelle'. I played dumb. They produced phone records that included dates, and the time and duration of all calls. They were all recorded. Michelle also sent me a card with two teddy bears broken up by love hearts, saying, 'I'm missing you, this place is not the same without you. Put in a half sheet if you want to come back to see me. Kiss, Kiss'. It was signed M. They took the card off me and said, 'We're keeping it'.

"I told them it was my private property, but they wouldn't give it back. They put me away in a small cell for hours. Then they took me back to the office and pinned me down by my throat on the edge of a table and said, 'You little bastard, you little cunt. You little English bastard'. I couldn't breathe. They asked me about what was in The Star. I said, 'Didn't you read it?' They said 'no' I told the two officers that she (Michelle) was in my cell masturbating me. They said, 'No she wasn't'. I said, 'Yes she was'. They repeated, 'No she wasn't' and it kept going on like that and it was leading nowhere. I just wanted to get out of there. After three-and-a-half hours, I said 'No, she wasn't'.

"An officer on the bus on the way down to Portlaoise said he *knew what it was all about. For months my cell was searched two and three times every week. You normally only get searched every three months. I told an officer that they had better stop searching my cell or I'd take them to the High Court for harassment and racial discrimination.*

"He said the book recorded that my cell was only searched every couple of months. They used to open my TV to see if I had a mobile phone hidden there. They would make me pull down my boxer shorts, which is illegal and look up my rectum. All they ever found in my cell was a battery for a mobile phone. They never told me why I was transferred from Mountjoy to the Midlands Prison, but some officers commented that I was right in what I did. I spoke to a friend in Australia and when she asked why I was transferred I told her. I had no reason to lie. Some days later the Governor called me up and said that I wasn't permitted to call that Australian number anymore. I asked, 'Why?' and he said it was because I was talking about my affair. I told him that I was telling no lies. Then an officer told me to be careful that the authorities were listening in to my phone calls all the time. I got abuse off some officers like, 'You cunt, why did you get her sacked?' I replied I did nothing wrong.

"Michelle asked me to come see her when I got released. I just said 'yes' to everything. I was keeping her sweet. Anyone in my position would play along. I don't feel a thing for her. If she knocked on my door I wouldn't even answer it. I don't want to have anything to do with her."

Craig said he had made quite a number of friends while serving his time in both Mountjoy and the Midlands Prison, and he would consider coming back to Ireland to visit.

"The day I was released my parents were waiting for me and strange as it may seem we took a holiday in Ireland. We went down to Kerry and visited all the usual tourist sites including Kate Kearney's Cottage. We really enjoyed it."

Craig says his parents are big fans of Foster and Allen and have most of their CDs.

We downed a few pints of beer at the Ibis Hotel before Craig walked with me to the train station. He talked about his family and his new girlfriend. He told me she had been married before and he wondered was that good or bad!

As we parted at the train station, Craig Helliwell shook hands with me and said, *"Thanks for listening to me"*, before finally joking, *"And if you bump into that prison officer, tell her I wasn't asking for her."*

****

Over the years I gave many of my contacts star ratings because of the quality of the tip-offs they supplied. As members of the media, we couldn't survive without our contacts, and I'm one journalist who tries to make sure that they know I appreciate them. To say *"thanks"* costs nothing, but it means a lot to people, as my good friend Jack McGuinness used to say.

Of course there is nothing as bad as the guy who comes up to you half-pissed in the pub and says, *"Jaysus I had a great story last week. I was going to ring you."* That, of course, is after the story has broken and it's too late...

On one particular occasion one of my five-star contacts told me that if I called to see a David Bainbridge in County Laois I'd get a good story.

I should have asked him what the story was about, but the reason I didn't was simply because I thought I knew what the gist of it might be. I knew that David Bainbridge had been through a terrible tragedy some six or seven years earlier. His wife Patti had been blasted to death at point-blank range by their 29-year-old mentally disturbed son Nigel. So as far as I was concerned, Mr Bainbridge was probably anxious to talk about the terrible tragedy that turned his life upside-down.

The couple had come from England in 1986 and purchased the Old Rectory at remote Coolrain, near Mountrath in County Laois.

David's wife Patti was Irish, having emigrated to England in 1951 as a teenager, and the couple had met in England. The Bainbridges had hoped to renovate the Old Rectory and sell it on for profit. They remained in England but made frequent trips to Coolrain to work on the renovations.

It was on one of those extended trips to County Laois that tragedy struck.

Nigel, their youngest son, had been unwell and acting strangely and the couple brought him from England to stay with them. On one occasion, while living in Paris, he had been found naked in the River Seine.

The move to Coolrain brought no improvement, his father David would later say. Nigel behaved like a recluse, spending long periods alone in his bedroom. He would eat only food he had prepared himself.

As Nigel's condition continued to deteriorate his mother Patti refused to have him committed for treatment. A local doctor was very concerned and said he should be treated for possible paranoid schizophrenia in a psychiatric hospital. But neither Mum nor Dad would sign the necessary papers. Patti was particularly reluctant to have her son detained in a psychiatric unit.

On May 6, 1996, Nigel Bainbridge took his father's .22 rifle and shot his mum Patti (61) in the back at point-blank range. As the mother-of-three lay bleeding to death on the kitchen floor, Nigel phoned Mountrath Garda Station. The man who answered the phone was popular Garda Sergeant Jim Arthurs. *"Hello Jim, I'm after shooting my mother,"* said the man on the other end.

When gardai arrived at the house they found David Bainbridge out mowing the lawn and totally unaware of the horrifying killing of his wife that had just happened inside the house. As Sergeant Arthurs shouted to David that there had been a shooting, Nigel ran out the front door shouting, *"I killed her, she was poisoning my mind."*

Sticking out his tongue, which was green-coated, into Sergeant Arthurs' face he went on: *"Can't you see she's poisoning me?"*

When gardai tried to arrest Nigel Bainbridge at the scene he struggled and kept roaring: *"Bastards. She's dying, get an ambulance, you're wasting time."* Realising his wife was dead, a distraught David roared at his son: *"You bastard, you've killed her."*

During the murder trial at Dublin's Central Criminal Court, there was medical evidence that Nigel Bainbridge was *"mad, out of it..."*

He was found guilty but insane and sent to the Central Mental Hospital at Dundrum. Nigel Bainbridge said he did not intend to kill his mother. Describing her as *"warm and gentle"* he added that the killing occurred during *"a moment of madness"*.

It was around noon when I arrived at the Old Rectory in Coolrain on April 4, 2003, accompanied by photographer James Flynn. James decided to stay discreetly in the car while I approached the front door. I was still wondering what story exactly might be told.

I knocked on the door three or four times. There was no reply. I decided to go around the back of the house hoping that there wasn't a wicked dog around. I noticed a tall woman standing near the back door tending to flowers and shrubs in the tiny, but rather neat garden. Wearing a long grey dress she seemed a bit worn or, as we'd say in the Midlands, *"haggard"*, but she still managed a smile.

"Good morning. I am looking for a Mr David Bainbridge," I said.

"I'm him," she said.

I honestly thought I had not heard her reply properly so I repeated that I was looking for Mister Bainbridge.

"Yes, I'm him, and don't look so surprised. That is what has you here, isn't it?" she said, smiling.

"Jaysus," I murmured to myself. I was flummoxed. I didn't know what to say next. *"I don't understand,"* I said.

She invited me in. Staring me straight in the eyes she repeated: *"Don't be pretending that you didn't know I had a sex change. That is why you are here."*

Still trying to come to grips with my situation, I assured her that I didn't know... What I did know was that I was after landing myself a good yarn and I wasn't about to let it slip.

"Well, you are not the first and no doubt you won't be the last to have one," I said, trying to bring a sense of reality and normality to the situation.

She/he then spoke freely to me in a wide-ranging interview for my newspaper, and consented to be photographed by my colleague James Flynn. My interviewee said that she only got freedom after the sex change operation. Now calling herself *"Melanie"*, she went on to say: *"I have freedom from something I suppressed most of my life."*

She said she was now aged 69 and told how she had been living a lie as a male for most of her life including the 38 years she had spent with wife Patricia — there were three sons from the marriage.

There was no offer of tea, but she was otherwise very hospitable. Gazing at a picture of late wife Patti, my hostess/host added, *"It was my love for her, for Patti, who was every-*

thing to me, that helped me bear the hidden pain. When I lost her, I lost everything."

By this stage I was sort of coming to grips with the situation and perhaps feeling a bit sorry for her/him.

Reminding me again that her name was now Melanie, she continued to say that it was Nigel's foul deed that finally drove her/him to have a sex change.

"I felt that doing what I did helped me to get away from the man, the person that had been through all the trauma of losing one's partner," Melanie said.

"For a long time I couldn't forgive Nigel. Now I do. Now I understand that he wasn't well when he shot his mother."

It was three years after the tragedy that David Bainbridge, at the age of 64, booked into a private London clinic, London Bridge Hospital, for the £10,000 (sterling) surgery.

Back in Ireland, Melanie's simple rural neighbours found it hard to come to terms with a man turning into a woman — it made for great conversations in the local pub in the evenings and in the back seats of the local church on Sundays.

Melanie, who was almost 70 years old at the time of our interview, said she had experienced a normal enough boyhood back in England and played soccer and cricket with the all the local teams.

But she said that she always knew she was different, that inside there was another person trying to get out. That inner contradiction came to the fore as a result of the terrible tragedy that unfolded in the kitchen of the Old Rectory at remote Coolrain near the Slieve Bloom Mountains.

It made a great article for the *Irish Daily Star*. I was most grateful to my contact for steering me in the direction of a marvellous, most unusual story. But when I next bumped into him, I could not resist having a go at him for landing me in a rather challenging situation without any warning. He explained that if he had told me the full truth I might never have called around to the Bainbridge home, and missed out on the story. Maybe he was right!

CHAPTER 12

Tragedy Beyond Words

THERE is one story that has stayed with me from day one and I doubt it will ever leave me. It haunted me for months and months and each time I drive through the town of Portarlington I relive it all over again. I had just got off a flight from Amsterdam on a sunny Sunday morning. It was the June Bank Holiday weekend and I was looking forward to relaxing for the couple of days. Anytime I'm away I love to grab the news on arrival home and the first thing I do when I get into the car is switch on the radio. It was just past the hour when I tuned in that Sunday morning, June 3, 1996. I was too late to get the entire story but I did grasp the fact that members of a family had been lost in a devastating house fire. I didn't know where, but something told me it was in my area. I had to wait an hour until the following news bulletin to get the story in full, and by this time I was near home. The fire had been in Portarlington, just up the road from my home and the Maher family residence had been destroyed. The fire had taken the lives of several members of the Maher family.

I called the *Star* newsdesk and Bernard Phelan was on duty.

He hadn't many details at that time but he seemed happy when I told him I'd look after it. Little did I realise that I'd be there for a number of days and would be covering the funerals. I had not known the family personally but I was aware that one of the family, Colm Maher, had played senior football with Laois. Before I reached Portarlington I was now aware that the fire had taken the lives of Breda Maher (49), her two sons and three daughters at Marian Hill on the outskirts of the County Laois town, and a third son was critically ill.

There was a huge crowd around the area when I arrived and everybody was ashen-faced. People were walking around like zombies. Journalists from every major publication in the country were assembling and TV satellite dishes were beaming out the pictures across the world. I went to the local East End Hotel where some media had assembled. It was there I spoke with local GP Dr Adrian Honan. At this stage the fire had claimed Breda Maher (49), and her children Mark (24), Barry (12), Joanne (8), Fiona (6) and Martina (2). Another son, Colm, was still fighting for his life in a Dublin hospital. Dr Honan told me Colm's chances of survival were slim. He was right. Colm died the next day. He had been the hero of the tragedy. Colm had got out of the burning inferno and was on the lawn outside the two-storey dwelling when some shouted that little Barry, a 12-year-old invalid, was still upstairs. Colm dashed back into the house, climbed the stairs, grabbed young Barry and was on his way back out when the stairs collapsed. Young Barry died at the scene. There are two things in particular that will always remain with me and that was the dignity of Alo Maher and his surviving sons. This was also remarked upon by then President of Ireland Mary Robinson when she visited the family some weeks later. I have never been able to remove from my mind the memory of the evening that the remains of the family were removed to St

Michael's Church. Watching Alo Maher wheel out the coffins one after the other and finally the two white coffins of little Fiona (6) and Martina (2) still haunts me. It was the first time in my journalistic career that I broke down. Hours later a copy-taker at *The Star* said to me, *"Are you going to make us all cry again tonight?"*

A nationwide trust fund set up by the GAA for the Maher family reached a staggering €630,000 (£500,000) within four weeks. I remember phoning Alo Maher to tell him that the fund had reached half a million. There was a pause on the line and then in a low quivering voice he said, *"Thanks Kevin, but do you know there were many nights here when Breda and I scraped together the price of a drink, but we were so happy."* Local GAA chairman Joe O'Dwyer spoke of the closeness of the Maher family, and recounted one event when Breda Maher had her first daughter, Joanne. *"You wouldn't see it in a film, but when Breda was coming home from hospital with the first little girl all her sons formed a guard of honour from the kerbside up to the front door of the house. It was really lovely. That's the sort of a family they were."*

Alo Maher died in 2008, leaving behind his sons Alo (jnr) Paul, Vincent, Brendan and Dominic.

****

It took me almost a year to come to grips with the terrible house fire tragedy in Portarlington, Co Laois, in June 1996 that claimed the lives of Breda Maher, her three sons and three daughters.

I had hoped that I would never again have to cover such a tragedy, but I knew that in this business that was asking too much.

But the experience of covering that terrible week in

Portarlington did not prepare me for the next one. It was 10 years later when I was detailed to a fire tragedy at a halting site in Dublin's Clondalkin estate. All I knew as I drove away from the *Star* office in Terenure was that there had been a bad fire and the first reports indicated that a child had died.

But nothing could have prepared me for what I faced when I arrived at the halting site at the Nangor Road that day. Men, women and children were screaming aloud. There was mayhem. Some were hugging each other and crying uncontrollably, while others wandered in and out through the caravans like zombies.

Then I noticed that the majority of the inhabitants of the site were gathered around one particular caravan. I made my way towards this caravan wondering what I would or should say. Have such words been created yet? I'm sure the last thing they needed were some intrusive journalists asking stupid questions.

One young girl was standing outside the caravan and she came to meet me. *"Are you from the guards, sir?"* she asked politely as tears streamed down her rosy cheeks.

I told her I was from a newspaper and that I was so sorry for her loss. I asked her what had happened. It was only then that I realised that not just one, but two little children had perished in a caravan fire. Tots Michael McGinley (3) and his 18-month-old brother Joe had perished when their caravan had been engulfed in flames.

The children's mother Lisa had been in hospital having treatment for a skin problem and their 24-year-old aunt Anne McGinley had been taking care of the children.

This young girl invited me inside the caravan and introduced me to the children's grandmother, Winnie McGinley (49). The heartbroken grandmother sat clutching a picture of her dead grandchildren and invited me to join her on the couch.

She was shaking, but shook hands with me. I told her I was so sorry. *"Get the man a mug of tay,"* she ordered one of the younger ones.

Still clutching that picture of the two little boys, Winnie McGinley cried uncontrollably and told me, *"My two little grandsons are gone all because of more discrimination against Travellers. Discrimination even on a Travellers' site,"* she wept.

She was also angry and said that they were living in worse conditions than Travellers endured decades ago because the South Dublin County Council had forced them off their original bay on the halting site at Nangor Road in Dublin's Clondalkin. She added that there was no power supply, no proper toilets and an insufficient water supply on the site where the tragedy occurred.

Gran McGinley said they had no alternative but to re-connect a power supply from another unoccupied halting site. Young Anne McGinley had only left the caravan for less than two minutes to get water from a nearby washroom. When she returned and opened the caravan door the place erupted into a fireball.

Although badly shaken at the time, Anne made several attempts to save her two nephews but was beaten back by the thick smoke, the flames and the intense heat. She had managed to pull a window from its frame but was unable to get Michael McGinley through the opening. Little Joe was strapped in a baby seat.

Before I left the site that morning, Winnie McGinley asked me to return that evening. I promised her I would, and when I returned, the children's mother Lisa was there. Travellers from around the country had now gathered in their hundreds at the Nangor Road halting site, with hundreds more expected to arrive in from England for the funerals.

I was then introduced to the children's mother, Lisa

McGinley. We spoke briefly. With darkness descending over the Nangor Road site, Lisa walked with me from her sister's caravan in the direction of the caravan where the children perished. There was an eerie atmosphere. I wasn't looking forward to this. But as the charred remains of the caravan came into view, Lisa stopped, gripped my arm and broke down crying.

"*They are gone. They are gone forever. Oh God, oh my God what am I going to do?*" she sobbed.

Her cries were ringing in my head for weeks afterwards. I asked myself over and over again, how could anyone, journalist or not, be indifferent to such a situation?

****

Life on the road as a newspaper hack wasn't always immersed in such tragic circumstances. I remember one time there was great excitement in our office when I approached the newsdesk and told them that a son of the man known as "Comical Ali" was working as a surgeon in a Dublin hospital.

Saeed Al-Sahaf became the best-known face on TV during the first three weeks of the 2003 Iraq war, when his incredible spins on the Iraqi position saw him dubbed "Comical Ali". A press spokesman for the Saddam Hussein regime, Comical Ali was claiming that the US forces were about to surrender even as the international media, and the whole world, knew the Americans were taking control of Baghdad.

We decided to keep the yarn as quiet as possible and when I received information that Comical Ali's son Osama was stationed at Dublin's Beaumont Hospital we decided to stake him out. We thought it would be unfair to approach him in the hospital and it would also give him an opportunity to hide from us. We received further information that he was living nearby, that he walked to work, and as far as identification was concerned he was a double for his dad. So we sat and we watched and it went on for days. The powers-that-be were getting a bit sceptical but I was adamant that I was going to get him. I failed. I decided to phone him at the hospital and ended up getting through to his voicemail. I left a message that I wanted to talk to him. Within 24 hours he returned my call, and he was very surprised when he discovered that I was calling from the *Star* newspaper. I thought that if I asked him if he was a son of Comical Ali and he denied it, I had no proof. I would then be in an awkward situation, so I addressed him on the understanding that I knew he was a son. So I hit him with direct questions about his dad and his dad's role as one of Saddam's men.

Osama did not deny his father was Comical Ali. He told me: *"My father knows he is responsible for his own decisions. But as a father he is a good man. He is a very friendly guy. When he came home from work and took off his uniform we did not discuss his job."*

I found Osama to be a very nice man. He wanted to leave the memories of Baghdad behind and get on with his life as a doctor. He told me he had studied in Jordan for nine years but that he had worked in Baghdad hospitals for two years. He had witnessed the sufferings of the people first-hand and he laid the blame at the feet of the Americans and the sanctions imposed on Iraq before the invasion.

"Now I wish the people a good outcome and hopefully the past is all over and we can live in peace and harmony in a democracy," he said.

There were mixed reactions to Osama's father Comical Ali from Iraqi nationals living in Ireland. One Iraqi professional said: *"Saeed Al-Sahaf is not a killer. He is a former manager of a TV station. He would not be capable of killing anyone. He is a politician."* However, another Iraqi told me, *"He may not*

have killed with his bare hands but he was part of the murdering
government bastards."

****

A former colleague at *The Star*, Shane Doran, once described me as the Midlands Reaper. We were talking about stories and how we came across some of them. I recounted how I was the only Irish journalist in Lourdes when Monsignor James Horan died in 1986. There was an occasion in July 2001 when I was taking my wife to Galway for a weekend when we got a call to stop off near Moate in County Westmeath, where a man had butchered his wife and two children the night before. Then there was the time I took my wife to Agadir in Morocco in February 2002 and two Irishmen were drowned a few hundred yards from our hotel. There was another occasion in London when a row erupted in an Irish hall and I watched policemen kneeling on the back of an Irishman that they had wrestled to the ground. He later died and the family sued for damages. Of course the biggest story I was involved in was the night I went to cover the story of a young girl who had been kidnapped on her way home from school. As already outlined, within half an hour of arriving in Moate, I had personally found her and handed her over to the Gardai. It was great, for a change, to cover a happy story rather than a tragic one.

CHAPTER 13

'Why Are You Killing Me Daddy?'

IT WAS a real hot Saturday at the end of July 2001 when my wife and I headed off to Galway for a few days. I had promised her this short break and I clearly remember her saying to me, *"If that phone of yours rings I'll throw it out through the car window. I hope it's turned off."* It is one of the hazards of the job but to be fair to Eileen she is most understanding and one of the best contacts I have ever had. She has a great nose for a story, and I sometimes think she is better at seeing a news angle than some journalists. Eileen's ears would prick up when she'd hear anything interesting. But I did get dirty looks when I received a call on the road between Tyrrellspass and Kilbeggan on that fine Saturday morning. It was a good contact on the other end. He told me that there had been a terrible tragedy at a place called Castledaly near Moate, and that a woman and two children had been murdered.

There was a gathering near the local shop and adjoining bungalow when we arrived. Within minutes I had established that a man called Greg Fox had murdered his 31-year-old wife Debbie and their two sons Trevor (9) and Killian (7). The couple had owned a shop and they were extremely well-liked in the area, and had been out the night before in the local pub. Debbie had gone home ahead of her husband Greg. When he got home a row between the couple ensued and Greg Fox stabbed his wife and left her lying in pool of blood. He then went upstairs to where his children were sleeping and he stabbed them to death.

We watched as State Pathologist Marie Cassidy arrived in a white two-piece suit and Eileen remarked that Ms Cassidy was better dressed for a ball than a blood bath. At first I thought that Hillary Clinton had arrived. Complete with shades she looked like Clinton's double. As she walked to the front door I could not help reflecting on the contrast between her elegance and the scene of slaughter she was about to examine.

In minutes she was going to be up to her ankles and elbows in blood. What she found that morning must have been one of the most horrific scenes she had ever witnessed. This man had slaughtered his wife and kids and their blood was still trickling through the house. Fox was found that morning in the family shop. He had some superficial injuries and was taken to hospital. He was later taken before a special sitting of Athlone District Court under an armed escort. There were concerns that Fox might be under threat after the tragedy unfolded, and the Gardai were taking no chances.

At the hearing he asked that he be locked up for 23 hours a day. His arm was in plaster and he looked gaunt as he trembled uncontrollably throughout the 15-minute hearing. He was later assessed at Cloverhill Prison and transferred to the Central Mental Hospital in Dundrum.

The people of Castledaly were so traumatised at the time that the then Midland Health Board set up a counselling service. Although the Fox family had only been in Castledaly for 16 months they had fitted in very well with the local community and daily chats with Debbie or Greg were always part of a visit to the store. The children were adored and the locals spoke of how mannerly the children were. Debbie had introduced the game of rounders to Castledaly and spent hours with local children in the GAA field that adjoined their premises. Greg Fox spent most of his time on the road wholesaling toiletries. Fox believed that his wife was having an affair with a local man and this is believed to be what the couple were rowing about when Fox flipped and attacked his whole family. I personally confronted the man named locally as the person Fox suspected of having an affair with Debbie. He said that he had no idea what I was talking about.

In November 2003 Fox pleaded guilty at Dublin's Central Criminal Court and received three life sentences. He revealed that as he inflicted fatal injuries on his son Trevor, the little boy said to him with his dying breath: *"Why are you killing me, Daddy?"* It has to be one of the saddest, most heartbreaking quotes ever to emerge from a murder case.

****

It was in February 2002 that Eileen and I decided to take a winter break in Morocco. On the plane were a group of employees from a leading Irish life assurance company, Acorn Life. We sat beside one of them and enjoyed his company on the four-hour flight from Dublin to Agadir. The company were holding a sales convention and the staff members were staying at the plush five-star Agadir Beach Club Hotel. We were staying at the nearby four-star Argana Hotel. We returned from the beach to the hotel around noon one day to find a note that had been shoved under our room door. It was from a Sunway Travel representative asking us to contact her. We both went pale and froze on the room floor. We were convinced there was bad news from home. With a shaking hand I called the representative and Eileen went and sat on the bed. The Sunway Travel representative told me that two members of the Acorn Life company had been drowned the previous evening. I immediately called our office in Dublin and Dave O'Connell was on the newsdesk. His first reaction was, *"Don't ever ask me to join you on a holiday."*

I went down to the Agadir Beach Club Hotel and there was an eerie silence in the restaurant where the Acorn employees were having lunch. I was greeted by a wall of silence when I entered. Even the guy who had sat beside us on the flight out was saying nothing. In fact he kicked the shins of his colleague when I turned to him for information. I established that Niall Sheridan from Athboy, a man in his mid-50s, and Joseph Bartley (25) from Navan had perished. The two County Meath men had been the recipients of awards from Acorn the previous day and had gone on the beer to celebrate their success. Unfortunately they decided to round off their celebrations that evening by hiring two jet skis. Earlier that day Eileen had remarked to me that the waves looked *"very angry"*. There was an elderly retired priest on the flight and he was staying at our hotel. When I told him about the tragedy and said the men were from County Meath and, as he was also from Meath, he would go down to their hotel. I bumped into him later that evening and he was visibly shaken. He told me that when he arrived at the hotel he discovered that he had actually officiated at Niall Sheridan's wedding many years before. There were emotional scenes the following weekend when we all assembled at Al-Massira Airport. Two passengers would not be joining us. Just seven days earlier they had gone out full of life and were looking forward to their week in the sun, only for it all to end in terrible tragedy.

****

One of the stories that I loved was when a man was deported to the wrong country. I know it was another yarn that infuriated the authorities and they tried to dismiss what had happened. It was a story of deportation, but with a twist. Thousands of euro was wasted on deporting a man to the wrong country.

The gardai who accompanied a non-national to West Africa to execute a deportation order in July 2003 were left red-faced when the authorities refused to accept the prisoner. The blushes got redder still when *The Star* splashed with the story and revealed how the prisoner in question had always insisted that he wasn't from Ghana. The three gardai who travelled to Ghana were forced to book a return flight for themselves and their prisoner and fly back to Dublin via Amsterdam first class. My informant told me that the non-national had told the immigration officers, not just once, but numerous times, before departing Ireland that he was from Liberia and not Ghana. On their arrival in Ghana the authorities said they would not accept the prisoner because he was not from there. The gardai, who were apparently booked into a hotel for three days while awaiting their return flight, then requested that the authorities hold the prisoner for them. This request was also denied and they were told in no uncertain terms to "get out" of the country and take their prisoner with them. On their arrival back in Dublin the non-national, whose name was George Victor, was taken to the Training Unit at Mountjoy Prison where he was held for a number of days before being released.

We learned at the time that the three gardai were somewhat disappointed by their embarrassing trip. "*They were really looking forward to a few days in the sun apart from the fact that they were jet-lagged after such a long journey,*" said our informant at the time. "*They were absolutely gutted when they were informed that the prisoner would not be allowed in, but then there was nothing they could do."* We had great difficulty in getting the Gardai to confirm our story and an email sent to the Garda Press Office went unanswered. When pressed they said that the email was forwarded to the Commissioner's Office but no reply had been received. But eventually the Garda Press Office confirmed that the Ghanaian authorities refused to accept the non-national claiming that he was not from their country. *"The documents were issued here, but our members were doing no more than executing the deportation order,"* said the Garda spokesman. *"They were left with no alternative but to put him on a plane and bring him back."* The Department of Justice then confirmed that the non-national had been taken to Ghana on foot of a deportation order but was refused entry into Ghana. The Department added that the mix-up was not on their side and they were in contact with the authorities in Ghana regarding the matter.

I was aware that George Victor had applied for asylum here before going over to live in London. He was arrested by British police and deported back to Ireland where his application for asylum was processed and turned down. The Department also confirmed that the non-national had been released.

Ironically, *The Star* had just weeks earlier exposed the amount of money spent deporting non-nationals from Ireland. In one case, 35 officers accompanied just 12 prisoners back to Nigeria at a cost to the taxpayer of €151,000. On another occasion five gardai used a private jet to take two people back to Algeria at a cost of more than €20,000. An amount of €190,000 was splashed out in March 2002 taking six failed asylum seekers to Lagos, Nigeria. Twenty officers went on that trip. The cost of staying at a five-star hotel in Accra, the capital of Ghana, such as the Labadi Beach Club, for B&B alone would cost in excess of €2,500 for the three gardai. The cost of the flights to Ghana, including the first class flights back home, would bring the total cost to almost €20,000. Legal costs in the George Victor case were estimated to have cost the State an additional €10,000. Remember that those figures relate to 2002 and 2003.

****

Journalists are said to be like gardai in that they are never off duty.

There is a lot of truth in that and I can personally recall that some of my best stories came about during holidays or on days off. Such was the case on August 24, 2006. I heard on radio that a man had barricaded himself into a house in Roscrea, Co Tipperary. As the day developed we learned that he was a man named Jim Hourigan who was threatening to blow up the house if gardai stormed it. His problems were complex. He had been sexually abused many years earlier in a religious congregation and he was also upset and angry over a drink-driving conviction. The Gardai had converged on the house as did large numbers of the media. The army disposal team were also called, with Jim Hourigan telling them that he had wired up eight gas cylinders. More than 40 people in the vicinity of his house had to be evacuated. The siege ran for hours and no-one seemed to be making progress. I obtained Jim's mobile phone number and decided to call him.

I identified myself to Jim and at first he said *"You are the same as the rest of them."*

I continued to talk to him and I asked him to tell me what exactly was bothering him. By now I had calmed him down and I immediately discovered that Jim Hourigan was an intelligent and articulate man. We spoke in detail about his past troubles and about a past that still haunted him. I told him that I understood his situation but at the same time I begged him to end his protest, and that no matter how serious his problems were they didn't warrant the taking of a human life. For more than 30 minutes he poured out his heart to me. He told me how while training to be a Christian Brother he had suffered years of sexual abuse at the hands of one of his superiors. Jim told me how depression had led him to drink excessively and this in turn created even more serious problems. He once spent two days in Limerick jail for non-payment of a drink-driving fine. He felt that his compensation claims for sexual abuse were not properly handled and that he had never received an apology from his abuser who was jailed for 18 months for abusing him.

Jim Hourigan told me he was sorry for what he had done, and for any shame he had brought on his family — but said he felt he could not take any more. The qualified electrical engineer had been on disability allowance since 1996.

"I'm not a violent man, and the gardai out there know that, but I will have to be guaranteed my rights," he said.

I told him; *"Jim, you have made your point. Please end your protest for your own sake and your family's sake."*

After a short pause he replied, *"Kevin, thanks for ringing me. I think you're a sound man. I think I can trust you. As soon as you leave down that phone will you say a prayer for me?"*

I promised him that I would and I kept a promise to meet him personally. We met a few days later in his native Limerick and on another occasion in Templemore in Co Tipperary after a District Court hearing. We had lunch in a local pub and we talked again at length about his problems. His problems were even more complex than I had anticipated. We spoke a few times after that on the phone before eventually losing contact with each other.

CHAPTER 14

Suffer The Little Children

MANY years before any State investigations into sexual abuse at Irish industrial schools and reformatories were carried out, I got a flight to Birmingham to meet a man called Ned Redmond. The 77-year-old Dubliner was anxious to tell me his story. He had spent three years locked up in two of Ireland's most notorious Borstal schools and he accused members of the Oblate religious congregation who ran the reformatories of turning him into a killing machine. The Oblates were made up of priests and Brothers — the boys often referred to them all as Brothers.

Ned Redmond described his first borstal, St Kevin's School in Glencree, Co Wicklow, as being similar to Colditz, adding that St Conleth's in Daingean, Co Offaly, was *"Belsen without the gas chambers"*.

Living in Birmingham with his wife Nancy, Ned had vivid and frightening memories of stomach-churning abuses against young boys, including abuse of a mentally handicapped child.

He watched young boys being stripped naked and flogged with a purpose-made leather belt until the blood ran down their legs and the flesh fell from their weak and scrawny bodies. He watched as one sadistic Brother rubbed coarse salt into the raw and bleeding wounds as the frail and often hungry victims screamed in agony before actually passing out with pain. Ned Redmond accuses the State of abandoning them to the mercy of the brutal Brothers who beat them at will to satisfy their own sadistic and sexual desires. This is Ned Redmond's shocking story as he told it to me at his home in Birmingham:

"I was born in Townsend Street in Dublin in 1924. I was one of two sons born to Christy and 'Snowball' (Nellie) Redmond. My father was away in the British army. We were very poor. We had nothing. It really was a matter of the survival of the fittest. In my area most of the fathers were either in the British army, working in England or were dead. There was no parental control. We just ran wild. We used to play football on the street and one day the ball went up onto the roof of the Bird's Custard factory. We climbed onto the roof to get the ball and through a skylight we could see all this jelly and custard. We were starving so we decided to break in and help ourselves. We were eating jelly out of the packets for a week.

"A few months later we were picked-up by the Gardai. At Pearse Street Garda Station while being questioned about stealing coal at the docks, we admitted the custard factory job. On January 26, 1940, six of us appeared before Judge Little in the Children's Court at Morgan Place. One received seven days at Mountjoy Prison's junior section, another received 14 days there because he was over 16 and the other four, including myself, were sentenced to three years at Glencree Reform School in the Wicklow Mountains. We were sentenced in the morning but we didn't arrive there until around five o'clock that evening. It was in the middle of winter. We were brought into an office and processed. We were starving. We had nothing to eat all day, but we got nothing there, only the allocation of a bed.

"The next morning all our clothes were taken and we were issued with a big pair of boots, a pair of stockings, a pair of corduroy trousers and a 'geansai' [sweater or jumper]. That was it. Nothing else. You had a little bag with a towel in it, a spare pair of socks, a spare shirt. You kept that with you throughout your time. They were laundered once a week. The reveille in summer was at 6.30am and 7am in winter. One of the kids was the bugler. There were 150 young lads in Glencree and we all slept in one dormitory. Each morning you went down a stairs and into a big wash house. There was a huge wooden trough in the middle of the floor with cold taps on either side. We lined up, 75 each side.

"After that you went to Mass. You went to Mass seven days a week and then to breakfast. After breakfast you went out into the square and waited there until the Brothers had their breakfast. You were then allocated your job. No idle hands. Everyone worked whether they were sick, sore or unwell. There was no hospital, no infirmary, no doctor's visits, and no visits from any Government department. No-one ever came near the place. We were just abandoned.

We had no books, no library, no reading material. I never had the chance to write home. We had no contact with the outside world. I used to pity the poor kids from faraway places. There was one chap there from Cavan. His name was Sam. He was continuously being flogged for nothing at all. They just seemed to pick on him for nothing. He was a great footballer, very tough. He wouldn't give in to them when they were flogging him. They loved for you to cry and beg for mercy. And they'd flog you until you did. A flogging was anything from six to 14 lashes across your bare backside. They'd pull down your trousers to your ankles. It was carried out either at night or in the dormitory when all the kids were going to bed.

"Sometimes it was done in the middle of the square with all the kids gathered around. It was always done in public so as to *frighten the others. The strap was about two-and-a-half feet in length, two inches in width and an inch thick. It was pure leather and purpose-made in the shoemaker's shop. Any Brother had the authority to flog you at any time he felt like it. But it was usually the head Brother, a Brother Kearns, that administered it. Your arse would be bleeding badly. There was a Brother Ahern there and he would then delight in rubbing coarse salt into the wound.*

"As you lay in bed the pain would eventually ease and through sheer tiredness and exhaustion you'd fall asleep. The Brothers then devised a new and an even more cruel method. They decided to flog you before breakfast so that you had to walk around all day with the rough material of the trousers rubbing against the raw flesh. For an infringement of the rules, even something minor, you were put on a diet of bread and water. That was a four-ounce slice of bread and a mug of water. That is all you got, three times a day, three days on and three days off for 28 days. I was never sexually abused, and I have to admit that I never witnessed it either, but it went on. I escaped from Glencree twice. Each time I gave myself up. You'd get some flogging for that because it made the Brothers look silly and incompetent. You would be taken out onto the square and stripped naked. Then your best pal would be forced to stand in front of you. You had to lower your head and place it between your pal's legs as he would be told to close his legs tightly on your neck so that you couldn't pull away.

"The Brother then flogged you until you screamed for mercy as the blood ran down your arse and legs and the skin was peeling off.

"About five months after the Second World War broke out, Glencree was closed and we were all transferred to Daingean. Fifteen Brothers came with us. There were nuns in Daingean when we arrived but they left within a week. When we arrived in Daingean a Brother Dunne was in charge. He was a right

bastard. We called him 'Louie the Lip' because he had a curled lip. He was a bad pill. They were so bad in Daingean that when they discovered we were eating the apples from the orchard they cut down the apple trees. The three men in charge in Daingean were a Father O'Connor, a Father Lynch and a Father O'Brien.

"O'Connor and Lynch were OK, but O'Brien was a pig. He delighted in lashing you. Later on we got a Father Fitzsimons as superior. All you had to do was look at him to know he was an evil bastard. In Daingean you were allowed one visit a month. But if you breached any regulation you were denied a visit. My mother, who was dying at the time, made it to Daingean to see me. When she reached the gate after making it all the way from Dublin they wouldn't let her in. I had broken some silly rule. On one occasion in Daingean while I was on the punishment diet of bread and water, Jim Ashe, God rest him, who was in charge of the 'turkey run' (feeding the turkeys) was caught slipping me some bread.

"He was taken before Brother Dunne who gave him an awful flogging that seemed to last forever. Dunne frothed from the mouth as he tore him to pieces with his leather strap. Jim was then sentenced to 28 days on bread and water. But he wasn't allowed to eat it in the refectory where the meals were served. He was forced to carry bread for the turkeys as well as his own bread and water and warned not to spill anything. After feeding the turkeys he was then forced to kneel in the turkey shit and eat his own bread and drink his mug of water.

"Living conditions at Daingean were appalling. There was no heating in any of the rooms except where the Brothers lived. You got one blanket in summer and two in winter. You'd be freezing in bed. There was no hot water. I never had a bath. During my two years and eight months there I never even had a shower. During the summer we were brought to the nearby Grand Canal for a swim twice a month. If you took sick there was never anyone to look after you. I remember one kid from Wexford, a chap named Cheevers,

dying in Daingean. They buried him almost immediately. We were never told how or from what he died.

"The work was hard. Winter or summer, kids were marched to the bog. Inner-city kids knew nothing about digging out turf, but they had to learn. We were locked up at 8pm all year round. The lights went out and you weren't allowed to talk. But you'd be so tired you'd fall asleep.

"On leaving Daingean I joined the army. The 6th Motor Squadron, but I was discharged within weeks when they found out I had been institutionalised. With three other mates we headed for Northern Ireland and joined the British army. I served around the world. I was afraid of nothing. I had been turned into a killing machine by those bastards in Daingean and Glencree.

"Do I forgive them? If I don't forgive them, then I'm just as bad as they were. If they are in Hell they are doing the Devil's work for him, just as they did in Glencree and Daingean."

****

Notorious paedophile Father Brendan Smyth, who died at the sex offenders prison on The Curragh just a month into a 12-year sentence, was linked to a catalogue of sexual abuses at an orphanage that I investigated for the *The Star*. It has been estimated that the Irish priest, over a period of about 40 years, molested more than 100 children in Dublin, Belfast and elsewhere in Ireland, as well the United States, before he was finally brought to book.

The accounts of sexual and physical abuse at the former female Industrial School in Newtownforbes, County Longford, as told by former inmates and local people are stomach-churning.

Local people remembered Father Smyth coming to the industrial school to give week-long retreats. In addition to addressing entire classes during normal school hours, Father Smyth hand-picked little girls who were taken to the parlour in the evening time. It was there that the sex beast would have his way with them for as long as he wished. One girl who was sexually abused by Smyth reported the incident to the nuns and showed them a semen stain on her dress. The girl was stripped and flogged and told never to say anything bad about a priest again.

Now in her early 40s and living in Naas, Co Kildare, she is one of the former inmates in the process of taking a case against the Sisters of Mercy. She spoke to me about her life with the Mercy nuns, who, she claimed, showed everything but mercy.

Father Smyth also preyed on young boys who served Mass at the convent chapel in Newtownforbes. He would take them to the cinema in nearby Longford town in his black VW Beetle car. *"The auld bastard would grope us going along the road,"* said a local man. *"Sure we didn't know what he was at. One particular lad got it real bad. His life was destroyed."*

According to people in Newtownforbes, there was a brutal regime at the orphanage where little girls were worked to the bone from an early age. Most were engaged in the school's commercial laundry while other chores included milking cows and cleaning out cow byres. Scrubbing the floors and walls of cloisters and dormitories was a daily chore before and after attending school. They were badly fed, poorly dressed and were constantly flogged for the most minor of misdemeanors.

"The nuns checked the beds in the middle of the night and if any girl had soiled the sheets she was dragged from her bed, flogged, and then made to lie on fresh nettles," said a former employee. *"It was brutal."*

None of the Sisters involved in the running of the Industrial School are still alive. I learned during our investigation that a majority of complaints were being made by former inmates who are now living abroad. This would make a lot of sense in that a lot of them fled the country on being released, or as one lady put it, *"thrown to the wolves"* at the age of 16. One former inmate has undergone several operations on her feet as a result of being forced to wear boots several sizes too small. Surgeons have since told the woman that there is nothing more they can do for her.

The children who were sent to the school at Newtownforbes were mostly from deprived backgrounds. A lot of them were taken there by their fathers particularly in the event of the child's mother dying. The orphanage, which was founded in 1878 and closed in the early 1970s, accepted babies in the 1930s. Most of the babies were born out of wedlock and locals say that such children received a terrible time, with the nuns constantly telling them that they were dirty and filthy and had to pay for the sins of their unwed parents.

A source said, *"You could hear the little babies bawling all night. They were probably hungry or extremely sick."*

According to those close to the school, children who were placed there accompanied by sums of money were treated well but children who came from poor and deprived backgrounds arrived at Hell on Earth. They were pulled from their beds at 6am and commenced scrubbing out dormitories, working in the laundry, milking cows and cleaning out byres, and then went on to school by 9am.

The source said, *"The food they received wasn't fit for pigs. All I ever saw there was scraps of bread. Only for local people sneaking them in food they would have died from hunger. Some days they got a stew for their dinner. Well it was supposed to be a stew. It was like a bowl of dirty water and it was usually cold before the poor little children got it."*

Local people also remember how badly dressed the girls were. *"Winter or summer they had calico dresses as light as a bee's wing and big heavy boots either too big or too small for them. They were never taught the facts of life or anything about the outside world. If they were standing near the gates looking out through the bars and a man appeared on the street they would run away shouting, 'The man, the man,'* according to a source who worked at the orphanage.

When the inmates at the industrial school reached the age of 16 they were turfed out on the road. An old man who lived near the former industrial school told me, *"We often wondered what happened to them. They came out like zombies. They were poorly dressed, had no money, no homes, and no known relatives. They were just thrown to the wolves after a life of hell. The shame is really on all of us, but we were too afraid to do anything."*

When I visited the convent during my investigation I received a nice welcome that included tea and chocolate biscuits while I waited on their spokesperson to arrive. That nun eventually arrived but as soon as I announced the purpose of my visit the atmosphere changed and no-one was willing to talk to me. I didn't even get to finish my cup of coffee.

****

My original story on Newtownforbes brought a huge reaction, particularly from former inmates. One of them was a woman called Gertrude Lodo (57) who had been in Newtownforbes. Her brother Patrick Kane (60) had been in two institutions including Dublin's notorious Artane Industrial School.

The brother and sister wept openly as they recalled how they were abandoned by their unmarried mother. They were sent to separate institutions which they described as *"Hell on Earth"* and this resulted in them being kept apart for more than 50 years.

Gertrude and Patrick were still trying to overcome their emotions since learning that they were brother and sister. They were also battling to come to terms with their stay in institutions where both were savagely beaten and where Patrick was sexually abused for years. Gertrude spent 16 and a half years in Newtownforbes before she ran away and got a job in the Mater Hospital in Dublin and eventually emigrated to London. Patrick spent his first 10 years with the Sisters of Charity in Fair Street, Drogheda, before being sent to Artane Industrial School. Patrick later served in the Curragh's No 3 Army Band, drawing on his musical skills as a former member of the famous Artane Boys Band. He was finally bought out of the army by a family who adopted him and took him to the United States, where he married and raised a family of three.

Both Gertrude and Patrick went in search of their mother, but when they found her in Finglas in Dublin she denied that either of them had a brother or sister. Even when Gertrude arranged for her brother Patrick to arrive at his mother's house in Dublin while Gertrude was visiting there, his mother denied that she knew him, although she had met him just a year earlier. Gertrude told me that on discovering she had a brother she was really anxious to meet him, and when her mother finally conceded that he too had been brought up in an institution, she was even more eager to meet him.

"I said to myself, 'If anyone can understand me, then who better than him?' When we did finally meet we hugged each other and then we cried and cried and cried for hours," said Gertrude.

Now Patrick and Gertrude exchange daily greetings across the Atlantic and have learned that their mother had another four children and that all six had different fathers. One of those was Angela, who was fostered at birth and although they never knew it, Patrick and Angela lived close to each other for many years in the Bronx, New York. Patrick Kane also spoke of the terrible abuse he suffered in both institutions.

He says that in Drogheda he was stripped naked by a nun and then held up by the arms and legs by four bigger boys while the nun flogged him until she was tired. His crime for this punishment was that he failed to control his bladder while he waited in line to use the toilet. He was nine years old. Patrick and Gertrude told me they were hoping to build the bridges and fill the gaps that have divided them for more than half a century. They realised it would be difficult and torturous, and they added that they can never forgive or forget those who were in charge of them in the various institutions or the mother who abandoned them at birth.

****

For another story for the *Irish Daily Star*, I interviewed another woman who had been in the orphanage at Newtownforbes. Marie Radford, who now lives in Devon, England, said she had been sexually abused by the village priest, who has since passed on. Mrs Radford said that Father Frank Prunty would pick girls up in his arms before running his hand up their dresses and feeling their private parts. She also told how one girl called Lizzie, aged 16, who became pregnant by a local man, was severely flogged by the nuns. *"She disappeared soon after that and any time any of us asked where she was we got a belt in the face,"* Mrs Radford told me.

Mrs Radford told how another young girl, Mary Murphy, burned to death while the rest of them helplessly looking on. *"She was working in the laundry and her clothes caught fire. The poor thing ran out in the yard. There wasn't a nun to be seen. We watched her as she burned to death. I can still hear her screams."* The former inmate said that she was flogged because her maiden name was Deveraux and she was accused of being a descendant of the Normans who invaded Ireland. *"They would tell me that the Normans caused great difficulties in Ireland, before flogging me. I didn't even know what they were talking about. They eventually made me spell my name 'Devro.'"*

She also confirmed that little girls were made to lie on freshly cut nettles if they wet the bed. *"We could hear them screaming in the middle of the night. It was awful. I still have nightmares,"* Mrs Radford said. She told how the younger ones who wet their beds were forced to wear the urine-soiled sheet cloak-like to school. According to Marie, several babies died there and all of them were buried in the middle of the night.

Marie, who was born in Dublin in 1939, was sent to Newtownforbes at the age of three. She was to meet her mother on her death bed in 1959. When she challenged her dying mum as to why she had put her into the Newtownforbes orphanage, her mother told her that she had written to the nuns trying to claim her back but had been informed that the orphanage burned down and the orphans were all dead. *"I have never gone back to Ireland since I left it at the age of 21,"* said Mrs Radford. *"I could never face Newtownforbes and I can never and will never forgive the nuns that were there during my 18 years."*

Covering stories like this gave me a sad insight into the dark recesses of a hidden Ireland of former times.

Postscript

And so I come to an end of this memoir, this account of my working life over more than 45 years. I have had the great privilege of working in show business and of meeting some great individuals, some of whom became household names. I have also had the privilege of working in journalism, which gave me the opportunity to cover some great stories in Ireland and abroad. To paraphrase the old newspaper slogan, *"All human life was there".* I will always be grateful for the love and support of my wife Eileen and my children during one of the most traumatic events of my life — my liver transplant. I hope that this account of my own experiences and my successful operation will give courage to those who are facing a similar challenge. And my thanks again to the medical and nursing staff who were there for me during a difficult time, and to the donor who gave me the gift of life.